A Twist of Faith

A Twist of Faith

*An American Christian's Quest
to Help Orphans in Africa*

John Donnelly

Beacon Press, Boston

BEACON PRESS
25 Beacon Street
Boston, Massachusetts 02108-2892
www.beacon.org

Beacon Press books
are published under the auspices of
the Unitarian Universalist Association of Congregations.

15 14 13 12   8 7 6 5 4 3 2 1

This book is printed on acid-free paper that meets the uncoated paper
ANSI/NISO specifications for permanence as revised in 1992.

Text design by Kim Arney

Library of Congress Cataloging-in-Publication Data

Donnelly, John.
A twist of faith : an American Christian's quest to help
orphans in Africa / John Donnelly.
   p.   cm.
ISBN 978-0-8070-0132-5 (hardcover: alk. paper)
1. Church work with children—Malawi. 2. Church work
with children—Africa. 3. Nixon, David. I. Title.
BV2616.D58 2012
362.73'2—dc23   2012001326

To my parents, Michael and Mary Donnelly,
and to my mother-in-law, Lois Markt,
for raising children well

Contents

Chapter 1

A Moment in an African Field

This was all new. The country, the people, the big sky, the red-clay road that was so narrow it seemed to have been built for bicycles. Just being in Africa made him want to praise the Lord, which he did frequently and with great feeling. David Nixon Jr., an evangelical Christian and a do-it-all carpenter from a suburb of Charlotte, North Carolina, couldn't have been more excited, or more on edge, as he rode in the back seat of a long white Toyota Hiace van into the African bush.

He was traveling deep into the backcountry of a nation he had first heard about only months before—landlocked Malawi in southeastern Africa. He was in the middle of nowhere as far as he was concerned, about an hour's drive west of Lilongwe, the country's quiet capital. And he was with five fellow American missionaries, including two friends who, like him, were on their first trip to Africa. They all come in the middle of the summer in 2002 with a loose plan to find local churches and work with them to help orphans. The six of them weren't sure if that meant contributing money and whatever expertise each of them had to offer, or if it meant diving in and doing it all themselves.

Nixon was of average height and weight: five foot eight, 165 pounds. He shaved his head every day so close that his scalp shone, a habit he had begun a decade earlier when he'd spent months living in a tent, studying the Bible, and trying to figure out how he would follow God's word. He had strong arms, a broad chest, a linebacker's shoulders, a booming baritone voice, and eyes that could be as playful as a child's or as stern as a drill sergeant's. He was not good at hiding his emotions. When he was having a good day, he was full of energy and vim, ready to attack life. When troubles got him down, his shoulders slumped as if he were Atlas carrying the weight of the world. Those dark moods would come and go, but they didn't stay as long as they had when he was a young man hounded by trouble. He attributed the elevation of his mood to his trust in God. God was his Father, and when Nixon said grace, he praised God so thoroughly that the food would often get cold.

On this day in a field in Malawi, he felt vaguely like one of those explorers from a distant era. But he and his partners weren't looking for gold or diamonds, or for tribes that had had little contact with the outside world; they were hunting for a community in dire need of help. These men knew every community could use some assistance, so they needed to find a local organization they could feel comfortable with to act as their on-the-ground contact. They believed fervently they had to do all the good they could do for poor Africans, the polar opposite of the goal of most of those who'd come before them, decades and centuries earlier—people who wanted to pillage the continent's riches or enslave its inhabitants.

Their mission couldn't have come at a more urgent time. According to estimates put forth by the United Nations, in recent years the number of orphans in Africa had grown to 34 million, a huge jump from a decade before, due to the AIDS pandemic, which had hit sub-Saharan Africa with greater force than anywhere in the world. In 2002, AIDS treatment was available to people in wealthier countries but to only a tiny percentage of HIV-positive people in Africa, Latin America, and Asia. Just fifty thousand out of the millions of HIV-positive people in developing countries were receiving life-extending treatment. As a result, mothers and fathers in Malawi and throughout Africa were dying at alarming rates. Every day across Africa, relatives carried thousands of their near-to-death loved ones to hospitals that had no supplies or medications to save them. Hospital morgues stacked bodies in refrigerated and unrefrigerated rooms. The international community was just beginning to mount a response to this humanitarian emergency, forming the Global Fund to Fight AIDS, Tuberculosis, and Malaria in 2002; in 2003, the Bush administration committed billions of dollars to an ambitious program called the President's Emergency Plan for AIDS Relief, or PEPFAR.

But government programs and the continued work of well-established charities and nongovernmental groups that had labored for decades to deliver aid on behalf of wealthy nations weren't the only responses. Mostly hidden from public view and rarely recorded or tracked by government or independent evaluators, thousands of private American groups, the vast majority of them faith based, were stirred to action. According to academics who studied development assistance, those faith-based groups gave several billion dollars a year to African causes, a stunning amount that likely surpassed the contribution of the U.S. Agency for International Development's funding of African projects.

Over the past decade, I've often crossed paths with this underground movement of mostly untrained aid workers who arrived in countries across Africa. Five years ago, I decided to take a much closer look. In the fall of 2007, supported by a global-health reporting fellowship from the

Kaiser Family Foundation, photographer Dominic Chavez and I started to document what exactly was going on with the torrent of American do-gooders traveling around Africa to help children. I wanted to determine if these disparate efforts were making any difference, either positive or negative. I decided to go to Malawi first, a country I knew well from previous visits for my newspaper, the *Boston Globe*. And from the moment I started my journey, I saw American do-gooders everywhere. They were on every plane trip I took. In African countries, I ran into them at shopping malls, in government offices, in bars and restaurants at the end of long days. Usually within the first ten minutes of conversation, they brought up their deep Christian faith. More often than not, they extended an invitation for me to come see their work firsthand.

I also spent hours with the U.S. embassy employees who were the architects of the massive American response to fight AIDS. These were some of the most dedicated government workers I have ever met. In the early days of the PEPFAR initiative, they all seemed to work sixty or seventy or eighty hours a week. They were so dedicated because they knew the better the job they did, the more lives they'd save. There was no doubt in their minds. How could there be? If you lived in sub-Saharan Africa in 2003, all you had to do was go to a morgue or a coffin maker's shack or the adult wing of a city hospital to be confronted by the inescapable truth: AIDS was destroying the population of young adults in Africa. The PEPFAR workers were fascinated by, and sometimes more than slightly uneasy about, all the private Americans from faith-based groups who were requesting information or showing up at embassies asking how they could help African children. Several longtime U.S. foreign-service officers estimated that the number of private do-gooders was two to three times higher than it had been in the 1990s.

As the members of these faith-based groups boarded planes for faraway destinations like Lilongwe, Addis Ababa, Nairobi, and Dar es Salaam, they imagined themselves building orphanages. Some of them anxiously awaited the culmination of months of planning to be allowed to adopt parentless children. David Nixon's group from Monroe, North Carolina, was, in many respects, not so different from thousands of others. They were people with big hearts and big ideas. But like many of the others, they came without much else: without knowledge and, perhaps, without enough humility.

▲ ▲ ▲ ▲

Inside the van in the Malawi bush, Nixon videotaped the scene of their arrival—the road ending, groups of barefoot children chasing them, smiling and laughing and jumping and waving in the dust of the van's wake. The driver slowed the van to a stop, and Nixon hopped out. Trailed by children, he started to walk toward a clearing.

From the far side of the field, a group of Malawians appeared, walking and singing confidently and beautifully. They were singing in Chichewa, the local language, and their harmonies were so pleasing that the visitors stopped and let the group walk to them. Nixon began to talk as he shot video. He mustered all the composure he could to describe the obvious: "We just drove up and they started singing."

That was it. He could say nothing else. As the singers came closer, their voices rising, he tried to speak, but he couldn't. Ordinarily, he had the confidence and natural charisma to talk with anyone. He would look everyone straight in the eye and squeeze his or her hand firmly—as firmly as his own belief in God. He was earnest and evangelical, deadly serious and deeply committed, and he had the unshakable conviction that he was a crusading knight in a foreign land.

But as he stood listening to the singing villagers, his knees weakened, tears rolled down his cheeks, and a chill crawled down his spine. He believed at that moment he was in the presence of God. The thought overwhelmed him: *God stood with him.*

Why? Why now? Why here? What was it about that moment—about the group of Malawians, and the field, and the children who had gathered all around him as he kept shooting video? He didn't know. All he knew was that he had to do something on this ground. He had to do something to help these children. He felt that God was commanding him to do so. As he wept, he silently made a vow.

He was going to work in Africa, in this sliver of a country called Malawi that he knew nothing about, and he was going to help these beautiful children who had no parents. He was going to do good.

The path before him would never seem as simple and clear as it did at that moment. He was headed straight for trouble, and even though he had dealt with plenty of trouble in his life, this would test him—and teach him—like nothing had before. A twist of faith had brought him here. But to weather the trials to come, he would need strength, perseverance, and, most of all, an open heart and an open mind.

Chapter 2

The Road to Africa

David Nixon was born in Tulsa, Oklahoma, to parents who had both run away from their messy, unhappy lives. His father, David Nixon Sr., called Senior by many, was a long-distance truck driver, a no-nonsense man who had walked out on his first wife in North Carolina to move west with a raven-haired beauty named Elizabeth Lowe whom he'd met at a truck-company office in Baltimore. Just a few months after Elizabeth gave birth to David Jr., Senior took them on a circuitous monthlong trip across the United States in his big tractor-trailer truck, eventually ending in rural central North Carolina, not far outside Charlotte, where he had grown up.

The warm feelings from that trip unfortunately did not last. The boy grew up in a domestic battleground. The couple had a second child, a girl named Laura, and that only added more stress in the household. His parents' relationship moved from one volatile moment to the next: screaming matches, drinking to excess, breakups, makeups, and long periods when his father was on the road. At one point, his mother left his father, eventually divorcing him and taking David and his sister with her to Maryland. A few years later, his mother returned to North Carolina, moved back in with Senior, and remarried him, but it didn't get better. As a child, David knew to stay out of sight and keep his mouth shut when his father came home or when his mother had had too much to drink. From an early age, he learned to watch for signs of anger in his parents—a quick rejoinder or a sudden raised voice—and he would leave the room on those dark cues. But some things he couldn't avoid. Some things he was dragged into. And those were the particularly awful moments of cruelty at the hands of his father, events that were so painful and scarring that they would still be with him decades later.

One involved his pet Jersey bull, which he called J-boy. One day, when David was twelve, Senior told his son to bring the bull to the horse barn. The boy lovingly took care of the bull every day, feeding it grain and grass, talking to it, and stroking its ears. That morning, after David brought the bull to his father, Senior tied J-boy to a post, took out a rifle, and shot the bull in the head. As it crumpled to the ground, David froze. He wanted to shout at his father, to cry out, to pummel him. But he did none of those things. He just stood there. He knew if he said even a word, Senior would smack him so hard that he would hurt for days; that was what his father had done on other occasions of perceived disrespect. Senior saw his son standing there and curtly told him to help with the cutting, and soon the blood of the bull stained the boy's hands, arms, and chest. Senior told him that he'd killed the bull because a bull was a bull, not a pet, and David needed to learn that lesson. He said David was spending too much time with the bull, and that wasn't right. *A bull is a bull.* The words rattled around in the boy's mind. But David, even at age twelve, realized with great clarity that his father wasn't trying to teach him a lesson about a bull not being a pet; he was just doing what he wanted with no regard, and even contempt, for David's broken heart. Why else would he do it? For days after the killing, David felt he was spinning, knocked off balance, and he would walk for hours in the woods on his own with his .22 rifle. Growing up, David had always walked as part of his routine. Before his father killed J-boy, David used to shoot at birds or squirrels on his walks. He was a good shot and sometimes he would bring back enough dead squirrels for his grandmother to make squirrel stew, which he loved. But after the killing, he would shoot only at trees or rocks or the sky. Many years later, when he thought more deeply about the incident, he realized that from that day onward he never again shot an animal.

His father's meanness loomed over David's entire adolescence, but he managed to find solace at age fourteen, when he began to attend a nearby Southern Baptist church. The church's old school bus swung by their house on Sundays, and his mother agreed to allow her children to go to Bible study. Soon she too was lured into the church, and she started reading the Bible and taking her children to church on Sundays. At that first service, the preacher called for anyone who needed to be saved to come down to the front and be blessed.

David was so taken by the preacher's words that he made his way to the front with the others who wanted to publicly admit having sinned. He knelt before the preacher and he said the sinner's prayer and asked God for forgiveness. The preacher assured him, and thereafter at weekly Bible studies and Sunday's services, David opened his mind to the messages of God in the Bible. He listened intently to the preacher speak about the good in Jesus and the evil in Satan. He heard the description of heaven and hell every Sunday, and he found it helped him get his bearings in the world. He strived for heaven, but he feared any missteps would land him in hell.

The church teachings began affecting his mother, and David observed that she took the preacher's words literally.

One of the things preached at the church was that a Christian woman's role was to submit utterly to her husband, and so she started to do just that. David watched his mother blindly follow his father's demands, and it bothered him greatly. He wondered why anyone, much less a preacher, would tell a woman to obey a man who abused her and her children. So although his mother kept going to services, David stopped. He wanted to believe in God and in the hope of a more meaningful and fulfilling life, but if God demanded submission to a man as cruel as his father, he wanted none of it.

He was thrown off course by another set of events as well. During David's senior year in high school, his on-and-off girlfriend told him that she was pregnant and that he was the father. She gave birth to a boy; David and she married; and he dropped out of school just a few months shy of graduation. Months later, he enrolled in the military, one of the few options he saw for himself. At first it seemed to him that he had made a great choice. David had been a terrible student in high school, but he was nonetheless deeply intelligent. He scored exceedingly high on the army entrance exams, especially in math and questions that tested problem solving. His recruiter told him that if he performed well in his first months in the military, he could work on a top-secret project involving the nation's nuclear weapons.

It seemed his life was turning around. At boot camp in Fort Knox, Kentucky, his instructors praised him for his work ethic. They told him that with success came rewards. David thrived. He had entered the military weighing 120 pounds, but he started gaining weight, and in four months, he put on forty pounds of solid muscle. When he returned home after boot camp, his mother didn't recognize him. His sister said he looked like a bullfrog.

The military conducted extensive background checks on him and then gave him a top-secret security clearance, and he entered the nuclear weapons training program at the army's base at Redstone Arsenal, Alabama. His wife and their son joined him, but the relationship deteriorated. In some respects, it resembled his parents' in their early years. They fought horribly. David wouldn't return home until well after midnight some nights. His wife would sometimes disappear for a day or more.

David made arrangements with his parents for his wife and son to live in a trailer in North Carolina. In the meantime, he was assigned to a base in New Jersey, where he was part of a team charged with maintaining manuals for nuclear weapons and learning how to develop emergency measures to disable them. He roamed the New York City nightlife scene. A few months later, his wife told him she was pregnant with their second child, but David kept his distance. He wanted a divorce. He started dating another woman; he proposed marriage and she accepted. He adored her and her family. But this hope for a new life vanished as quickly as it had begun.

He was assigned to a base in Italy, starting in May of 1982. His fiancée broke off the relationship and not only because of the distance. She also had other issues with him. Nixon's life had crumbled again.

Just after arriving in Italy, as he unpacked his few belongings in the barracks, a group of guys approached him. One spoke for all of them.

"We need to know one thing," the speaker said. "Do you get high?"

David said he did. That started nearly two years of buying and dealing drugs, drinking heavily, and going to parties all over Italy, and it eventually ended what had been a promising career when military authorities caught him dealing drugs and dishonorably discharged him.

David moved back to the Charlotte area and found work in carpentry and plumbing. He was high or drunk most of the time, on pot or Jack Daniels. He loved the bar scene. For a time, he took a job as an exotic dancer at a Charlotte nightclub. One night, a friend introduced him to crack, and he went on a monthlong binge. Full days went by when he and his friend would do nothing but smoke crack and chase it with swigs of whiskey. By the end of those thirty days, he had lost his house and was living in his van with a Doberman and a wolf. He had no contact with his ex-wife and his two children.

He was twenty-eight now, and he wanted to find a way to stop the madness. He took his Doberman and wolf out to a large ball field to let them run and to let his mind wander. He finally called them in, put them in the back of his Chevy van, and drove off on a blacktop country road. He felt he could go no lower. He had done nothing with his life. He had thrown away everything he had. Every gain had been wiped out by his self-destructive behavior. He knew he had great talents and was capable of making his way in the world; he could handle any incident, knew how to size up people, always made the best of a given situation, and could solve seemingly any problems except his own. He could be a star at something. But he was also a jobless absent father who had just ended a thirty-day cocaine binge; he had nothing.

So as he was driving, he talked to God.

"God, if you are who I thought you were when I was a fourteen-year-old kid, before I got discouraged, before I got down and out, you need to let me know," he said. "You're the only hope for me. There's nothing else. There's nothing else worth living for."

He thought about all he had lost. "God, if you are real, please let me know," he said, tears streaming down his face as he drove. "There is nothing in this world that is really worth having if you don't have your sanity. If you are who I used to think you are, before all that has tainted me, you're the only hope, and I want to know if you are real. If you are real, I want to surrender. I need your help."

He heard a voice inside his head.

I am going to save you, the voice said.

He believed he was hearing God. He clutched the steering wheel hard and kept driving, stunned. Was he being saved? *Could* he be saved? He knew he had to get help, and he wondered who to turn to. He decided on his mother.

Over the years, Elizabeth Nixon had undergone tremendous changes. She had left Senior, stopped drinking, and committed herself to God. She realized that she needed to do something for herself. At age forty, she passed a test for her GED and received a high school equivalency diploma. Then she earned a bachelor's degree at Wingate College in North Carolina and went on to graduate school at Keene State College in New Hampshire. She took a job as a family counselor and worked part-time all the way through graduate school. At age fifty-one, she earned a master's degree in counseling and case management.

She was in New Hampshire when her son called. She told him she wanted to place him a rehabilitation center in Charlotte for thirty days. She called a counselor at the center.

"Can you give me this young man's address?" the counselor asked.

"He has no address," Elizabeth said.

"No address? Well, where does he live now?"

"In a van with a dog and a wolf."

The counselor paused. "I'll get right back to you. . . ."

Nixon moved into the Amethyst drug-rehabilitation center, hoping not just to cleanse his body of alcohol and drugs but also to surrender himself to God. That focus on spiritual and mental healing, he believed, would give him a foundation for staying clean.

Over the next several years, Nixon gradually rebuilt his life. He held on to his belief in God and his desire to serve the Lord, but he wasn't sure how to lead a true Christian life, whether that meant extending kindness to others in simple daily acts or following in Jesus's footsteps and devoting his life to God. He found several interesting jobs, including one at a division at Corning, a giant multinational company. Even though he had no formal training, he became a highly productive troubleshooter on fiber optics projects. Supervisors put him to work with Japanese engineers trying to optimize connections using fiber optics, and David spent days and nights at the lab, finding solutions that had eluded others. It was a trait that had begun to define him: if he was asked to solve a problem, he simply didn't stop until he found an answer, even if meant working at it for days on end. Despite his success at Corning, though, it became clear he would not get a promotion because he lacked a college degree. He was in a much better place than he'd been several years earlier, but he still dabbled with alcohol, and he found it hard to avoid the party scene. And although he'd briefly reestablished a relationship with his two sons, he wasn't able to sustain it.

He decided he needed another big change. He called up his sister, Terrie, owner of land near the old family home in Monroe, southeast of Charlotte, and asked if he could live on the land in a tent. She was puzzled, but she said yes.

Nixon set up a hundred-square-foot tent that had a dome in the middle and was tall enough for him to stand up in. His Doberman and wolf were gone, and his only companion was his gentle Rottweiler, Cole. He built a fenced-in area beside the tent for Cole, who slept next to Nixon at night. In the mornings, the two went for long walks in the woods.

He was thirty-four years old and he still hadn't figured out what he wanted to do with his life. He longed for simplicity, for a refuge from the complications that had come to define his life. He was trying to establish a relationship with God, but he felt numb most of the time. He wondered if he would ever feel the presence of God again; he decided that even if he didn't, he would still follow God because he knew now that God was real. He knew he wanted to be on God's side. So, for hours every day, thirty feet behind his old family home and with the woods at his back, Nixon read the Bible, especially the Old Testament. He kept returning to Job, to whom, more than anyone else, he could relate.

In the story of Job, Satan challenged God, telling him that Job prospered only because God had put a wall around him. Satan asked for permission to "touch" Job—to inflict great pain and see if Job would abandon God. God granted permission. A storm killed all of Job's children, and Job shaved his head, tore his clothes, and cried out, "Naked I came out of my mother's womb, and naked shall I return: Lord has given, and Lord has taken away, blessed be the name of the Lord."

Satan caused Job's body to break out in boils, and Job scratched his skin with broken pieces of pottery. Job's wife cursed God, but while Job questioned God as to why he was punishing him, he refused to blame God.

In his tent, Nixon found the Old Testament story came alive for him. He had shaved his head. He cried out and questioned what God had planned for him. He asked why so many bad things had happened to him, why he had squandered so many opportunities, why he had given himself up to addictions, why he had failed in his relationships with women, and why he couldn't harness his abundant talents to do some good.

The book of Job is ultimately a story about reconciling the existence of evil with the existence of a loving God. In his tent, Nixon put himself in Job's place. *Look at me,* he thought to himself. *What am I doing with my life now?* Satan believes he can make David fall. God says, Let's see what happens.

So what would happen?

God described to Job what it was like to bear responsibility for creating the world, and he asked Job, in a rhetorical sweep, whether he also had such an experience. In his speech, God emphasized his sovereignty in maintaining life in the world. He said he was king, and his subjects, including Job, had no place to question him.

All Nixon knew was that the Bible gave him more determination to follow God's word. He wouldn't curse God; he wouldn't question him. God was king, and he was his servant.

Nixon the servant wanted fellowship. He enrolled at the Southern Evangelical Seminary in Matthews, North Carolina, just north of Monroe. A Christian apologist had founded the seminary to present a rational basis for Christianity and to defend attacks on the faith. While Nixon was fascinated with the content of the classes, he believed the lecturers lacked passion and focused too much on intellectual approaches to the word of God.

He told one of the professors that God had spoken directly to him during that drive on a country road not far from Monroe. The professor scoffed at the idea. "If you think Jesus is talking to you, you need to write another Bible," he said.

A fellow classmate, a pilot who had worked in the African bush, supported Nixon in class. He said God had told him to fly to a remote village, and when he arrived he found dozens and dozens of people in dire need of his help. The professor said it couldn't happen.

Nixon dropped out after one semester. At the same time, his father had begun to tell him on a regular basis that it didn't look good for David to sleep in a tent every night—especially in plain view of the road. He offered to buy him a small camper, an offer Nixon accepted. The switch came just in time. On his last night outside, a freak windstorm swept through the area and shredded his tent. Once the clouds had passed, Nixon and his dog, Cole, looked up at the stars—and, he fervently believed, the heavens—until dawn.

The time in the tent and then the camper added up to two years. It was a period in which he built his faith, Bible page by Bible page, day by day, in his work and in his studies, and finally, after years of trials that went back to his boyhood, he felt he was a committed Christian.

Now he had a sense of God, but his spiritual understanding was not yet fully formed. Nixon believed that God was the Creator, but he wasn't sure about God's nature or what was in God's heart. God was his true Father; he had taught Nixon how he should act as a man, how he should conduct himself in business and in his personal life, but beyond knowing that, Nixon remained deeply puzzled about his place in the world and his ultimate purpose. He spent all that time in the tent and then the camper thinking about that, and he emerged without any sure answers, only more questions.

He moved into a house again, and he decided he was ready to join a congregation, hoping to find people as alive with the spirit of God as he was. On the recommendation of a friend, in 1997 he started attending Emmanuel Baptist Church in Monroe, which had been founded by just a few families less than two decades earlier. It now had a membership of about a thousand people and met in an arena-like building that could seat eleven hundred.

When he walked into the sanctuary, he could feel the Holy Spirit wash over him. He began to meet wonderful people, even though he saw cliques in the church and witnessed what he believed was bad behavior: some members lit cigarettes in the parking lot—a bad example for the children, the changed Nixon thought. He had come to faith later than most, and in those early months of joining a church he was like a wanderer who had returned to the flock feeling the purity of faith with much greater intensity, he felt, than those who had been attending church for years. He already had a firm basic view of what it meant to be a Christian: it didn't mean acting pious or not using curse words (although he didn't use any); it meant living according to one's convictions and sacrificing for others. He knew that most religions taught peace, honorable behavior, and the golden rule. He felt true Christianity was much more than that. It was laying down your life in an almost literal sense for people who might not know, or appreciate, that you were doing so. It meant living according to God's words, and living as Jesus did.

The pastor and elders took note of him early on. They could see his burning passion to spread the word of God. They wanted to take advantage of his enthusiasm and soon had him teaching Sunday school and speaking at a Wednesday-night Bible study for kids. Others in the church, hearing about his talent for fixing things and his vast energy, asked him to be on their church committees. He gladly joined a missions committee, which was tasked with identifying overseas work that the church could support.

Church members in the past had taken trips to help groups in Bolivia, and in 1999, Nixon joined a half a dozen others for an eight-day mission in Cochabamba, the country's third-largest city, with a population of about one million people.

Nixon's expectations were as high as could be. He decided he would fast for the duration of the trip—eight days—because, as he put it to a friend, "I just felt led by God to do it." The group worked on a couple of housing projects, handed out clothes, and got to know the city. But for Nixon, the pace was too slow. Some days, the volunteers didn't start until 10 or 11 A.M. And there seemed to be a lot of riding in cars and getting together for meetings. One day before four in the afternoon, the group stopped work to shop at a market that sold souvenirs. He didn't understand that. He wanted to work from first light until dark.

At the end of the week, the group had some money left over from what they'd collected from members of Emmanuel Baptist. The group had been working with two churches, and Nixon suggested dividing the remaining funds between the two. But the others argued that they should take the money back with them.

"You mean to tell me that we came all the way here and we're not going to leave the money we brought?" he said at a meeting.

Others in the group, including some deacons at the church, felt they had an obligation to bring any leftover cash back to Monroe and let the church leadership spend it. They won. Nixon felt it was one example among many of his being at odds with the group. He returned to North Carolina wondering if he really wanted to do any more mission trips. He wasn't sure they did much lasting good, and he felt he had different expectations than others did. It was an early warning sign that his goals were not in sync with those of his peers at the church.

Nixon, who had developed a thriving construction business, remained active at the church, stayed on the missions committee, and regularly attended a weekly Christian businessmen's lunch at the Hilltop Restaurant in Monroe. At one meeting in early 2002, the main speaker was John O. Danford, who lived in Monroe and worked at a local hospital as a patient representative. Starting in 1985, through his home church in California, Danford had been going on mission trips to Malawi, a narrow sliver of a country in southeastern Africa.

As Danford spoke, Nixon moved to the edge of his seat. Danford talked about planting the seeds for doing God's work among Christians in Malawi. He talked about how Malawi was one of the poorest places on earth. About how people were friendly, how they spoke English and welcomed foreigners. About how hard they worked. It was as if Danford had known exactly what Nixon was seeking and was methodically ticking off each of his requirements. Nixon wanted a place where the local people felt as passionately as he did about applying faith to good deeds and helping the most vulnerable people around them. He wanted a place that was desperate for assistance, that didn't have aid groups working in every village and town. And he wanted a place where he could logistically get things done; Malawi was small and most people spoke English, and these were additional signs that this was an area to explore as a possible start for his mission work.

After the talk, Nixon approached Danford and asked if they could meet to discuss Malawi further; he asked if Danford could also speak with leaders at Emmanuel Baptist

Church. Danford agreed to meet with Nixon and to speak to the deacons at Nixon's church.

In a burst of inspiration, Nixon reached out to Marvin Tarlton, a good friend and the chairman of the missions committee. Shortly after one Sunday service, Nixon approached his pastor, Jack Hildreth, about Danford's mission. Nixon said that he would like to travel with Danford and that he was hoping the church would support his trip and see it as a possible place to start a mission for children. He said Tarlton also was thinking of going.

As he talked with his pastor, Nixon saw another friend listening in on the conversation. It was Jimmy Baucom, a big, brawny guy who was as gentle as he was physically imposing. Nixon enjoyed Baucom's company, and he caught his eye during the conversation with Hildreth.

"Brother, have you ever thought about going to Africa?" Nixon asked Baucom.

"No, absolutely not," Baucom said.

They laughed. Baucom continued. "What good ol' redneck from Union County would ever think about going to Africa?"

"Why don't you think about it?" Nixon said.

Pastor Hildreth also encouraged him to give it some thought.

"Well," said Baucom, "if God wants me to go to Africa, he will make it happen."

No one could disagree with that. So Baucom, who had never ventured much farther than Myrtle Beach, South Carolina, started thinking and praying about going to Africa. It was not a comforting idea. His wife, Stella, whom he had married later in life and who had seen far more of the world than he, encouraged him to do it. Nixon also kept encouraging him.

Baucom didn't tell Nixon about the wave of dread he was feeling. That would have been rude, and Baucom didn't want to hurt anyone's feelings. He loved his routines, and that meant being home with Stella. He hated traveling. He had never even had a passport; Nixon, watching him go through the process of getting one, could see that Baucom viewed it as a monumental task.

And yet, as Baucom kept saying to Nixon and himself, if it was meant to be, God would make it happen.

Baucom, a fire inspector by trade who self-effacingly called himself an "average person," came to a conclusion that surprised him: it was God's will that he go. The three from Emmanuel Baptist—Nixon, Tarlton, and Baucom—decided that they would all go to Africa. Baucom felt he was being led to do this and that he should at least make a good faith effort to go. He needed funds for the trip so he wrote a letter and passed it around to friends asking for their support.

He was shocked by the response. Nearly everyone he asked dug into his or her pocket or wrote a check. In two months, he had collected $2,500—enough to pay for his airplane ticket plus an extra $800 or so for the mission.

Nixon and Tarlton also raised money and pitched in from their own savings. The men's fellowship at Emmanuel Baptist chipped in $500 for the three to use in Malawi as they wished. Nixon had received an insurance settlement and he had $65,000 in savings. He even gave Danford $3,000 to defray a large part of his travel expenses. Danford would be traveling with his wife and a young woman who was a friend of theirs.

Nixon, Tarlton, and Baucom raised enough cash and received enough medical donations to fill four large suitcases with children's medicine, bandages, toothpaste, and other supplies to give away in Malawi. Even the luggage, bought for a few dollars at a local Salvation Army store, would stay behind in Malawi. With palpable excitement, they held a luggage-packing party about a week before the trip, during which they gleefully packed the piles of donated supplies into the suitcases.

On July 12, 2002, the six of them boarded a plane in Charlotte—Tarlton and Baucom both holding their first passports—and headed for Amsterdam, where they would have a one-night layover before flying to Johannesburg and then to Malawi.

For Nixon, who had traveled widely in Europe during his military days, the trip itself was not novel, so he focused on what would happen when the team arrived in Malawi. He had bought a digital video camera the day before, and he spent much of the first leg of the journey reading the manual to figure out how it worked, as well as reading the Bible. But for Baucom, getting on a trans-Atlantic flight was a nerve-racking experience. He had a window seat, and he tried to take it all in without seeming too frightened, but he was trembling inside. His experience wasn't so different from that of Africans who board their first flight to Europe or America. Nixon watched him study a screen in front of him that showed the plane moving ever so slowly across a map and laughed at his friend's amazement.

When they arrived in Amsterdam, the group checked in at the hotel where they would stay for the next twenty-four hours. For Baucom, everything was new information—even the fact that Amsterdam was part of Holland. Nixon laughed about the irony of a group of Christian missionaries spending the night in Sin City, home to legalized prostitution, brothels, strip clubs, sex shops, and marijuana bars. However, what made the biggest impression on the first-time travelers wasn't the red-light district but the thousands of bicyclists on the streets and sidewalks. The three of them almost got run over a few times, but they admired the country's reliance on bicycles rather than cars. They may have been in unfamiliar surroundings, but they were open-minded enough to appreciate the differences they encountered abroad.

The next day, as their plane came in for a landing at Lilongwe International Airport on an Air Malawi flight, the Americans were nervous and excited. They could see a wide expanse of savanna with few trees and innumerable bushes. Smoke rose in the distance. They passed over huts and small homes. Nixon scanned the terrain and soaked it all in. He strained to identify something familiar—a tree, a bush, anything that reminded him of Monroe—but nothing looked like home.

Once they picked up their bags and made it through immigration and customs, the three Americans walked out to deep crowds of people. Danford and his group were a day behind them, and Nixon and his friends looked for their greeting party in the crowd, afraid they wouldn't be recognized. Their apprehension was unnecessary. Nixon and his friends were among only a handful of whites to get off the plane, and their greeters immediately flocked to the *azungus*, as they called the white men. They surrounded the three of them, took their bags, and hustled them to their two minibuses. Half of the greeters climbed into one, while the other half took Nixon and his partners to the other— then handed Nixon the keys. Malawians drive on the left side of the road. Nixon nervously started the engine and drove off—not only on the wrong side of the road (from his perspective), but also while maneuvering a six-gear stick shift with his left hand.

He drove the minibus into the center of Lilongwe, which was a small capital by African standards. In 2002, the town had only one large supermarket. The commercial row on the main street consisted of a few banks, some money-changing outfits, booths selling phone cards, one or two hardware stores, and a couple of restaurants. People sold newspapers, pens, notebooks, extension cords, gum, maps, and scores of other items on the streets and at stoplights, where they besieged drivers, asking them to buy their wares.

An inordinate number of people on the streets were exceedingly thin, a frequent sign of acute sickness, most likely AIDS in this case. On a hilltop near the town center, hidden from Nixon's view, was the public hospital, then called Lilongwe Central, where on an average day four or five people died from AIDS. So many sick people came to the hospital that attendants directed newcomers to the wards' outside balconies, where some slept on the floor. These were the days before life-extending antiretroviral drugs were available to most Malawians, days when there were floods of preventable deaths.

But Nixon couldn't have known any of this at that moment. In fact, he barely registered the people on the streets, focusing instead on making sure he didn't hit anything. They finally arrived at a modest brick house that was owned by a short, stout retired businessman named Mr. Japhet Maliro and located in a lower-middle-class neighborhood called Area 25; this was where Danford always stayed on his visits. The Malawians brought them inside.

The hosts held a welcoming party of sorts and told their stories, mostly tales of woe. Nixon peppered them with questions. He listened intently, laughed along with them, called them "brother" or "sister" in his slight southern drawl, and the Malawians seemed to connect with him immediately.

But the get-together wasn't just a greeting. The local pastors wanted to press home a critical issue: a severe drought had ruined crops across the country, and an unknown number of people had already died from lack of food. Nixon and his friends were planning to buy bags of food at the market and deliver it to villages, but the ministers asked Nixon and the others for money now. They didn't want to wait for the food to arrive. They said that lives depended on it, and if the Americans waited a few days, dozens more could die. Nixon and his friends decided to give the pastors money immediately to buy food for people in their communities. Each of them dug into his pockets and gave the pastors the equivalent of a couple hundred dollars. The pastors were thrilled.

It was getting late, and the Malawians wanted to get home before dark, so they asked Nixon to drive them home. The three Americans and a large group of local pastors piled into one minibus, and they drove, and drove, and drove. Nixon started to worry that he would never find his way back. But this anxiety was soon flooded by a deep joy. The Malawians were singing gospel songs in beautiful harmony. An orange-red sun was setting, and Nixon, exhausted but exhilarated, suddenly had tears streaming down his cheeks. There was no stopping them. He felt he had entered a spiritual realm, with God by his side, inside an old minibus, driving on the wrong side of the road, sitting next to people who had been strangers just hours before. He could have driven all night, enjoying the moment, treasuring the spirit of God.

Chapter 3

Oprah: One of Many

She was dressed entirely in pink, wearing a floor-length gown, a fairy godmother equipped with everything but the wand. It was January 2, 2007, some five years after David Nixon's first trip to Malawi, and Oprah Winfrey looked radiant at the opening of her Oprah Winfrey Leadership Academy for Girls in the small town of Henley-on-Klip, about twenty-five miles south of Johannesburg, South Africa. She had spent $40 million on this academy, and this was its debut—the moment when she would tell the world how much she wanted to give to these girls, who, she said, were not so different from herself.

"I was a poor girl who grew up with my grandmother, like so many of these girls, with no water and electricity," Winfrey said. "I wanted to give this opportunity to girls who had a light so bright that not even poverty could dim that light."

At the opening, which also featured Nelson Mandela; singers Tina Turner, Mary J. Blige, and Mariah Carey; actors Sidney Poitier and Chris Tucker; and director Spike Lee, Winfrey welcomed 152 girls into the academy. They were all seventh- or eighth-graders, but in the coming years, the school would gradually add other grades, bringing in more girls.

In the United States, the reaction to Winfrey's largesse was mainly positive; many admired her heartfelt desire to assist these girls, not to mention her backing that up with millions and millions of dollars. Her few critics tended to ask why Winfrey didn't invest in children's education in the United States. Winfrey had an answer ready for that: she said that she could accomplish so much more with the money overseas.

When I heard Winfrey say this, I wondered how it could be true. Was she accomplishing as much as she could? I decided to call several people who worked for programs serving orphans and vulnerable children, or OVCs—an acronym that sounded oddly like a new brand of truck. When I told them the amount Winfrey had spent, several asked me to repeat it. They didn't believe their ears. A few gasped when I told them about the expensive extras in the school, including special duvet covers, a wellness center, dance classes, photography workshops, and cooking sessions from Winfrey's personal chef. Some said a gift to their organization in the amount of what it cost a single student to attend Winfrey's academy for a year would cover their entire annual budget; that sum could help hundreds, if not thousands, of students. At the time of the opening, for anyone who wanted to do the math, the cost per student was an astounding $263,158.

At the same time that Winfrey opened her academy, I heard from U.S. government sources that officials in the Office of the U.S. Global AIDS Coordinator were debating the fair annual cost of supporting an orphan or vulnerable child, including schooling, meals, and after-school programs. These small teams of experts had the advantage of comparing per-child cost across countries. The trigger of the conversation, I learned, wasn't Winfrey's school but rather what some considered to be a promising if pricey program involving grandmothers caring for orphans in the southeast African kingdom of Swaziland, only about 150 miles east of Oprah's academy. The cost of the program: $200 per child annually. That concern over price put Winfrey's largesse in proper perspective for me. If the experts thought $200 might be too high, it wasn't hard to imagine what they thought of Winfrey's project.

But some U.S. officials, including Ambassadors Randall Tobias and Dr. Mark Dybul, the first two leaders of PEPFAR, made the point that Winfrey was only the most public face of a largely hidden army of American volunteers who worked on projects to help African children. Dybul was involved in PEPFAR from the start, working as a deputy to Dr. Anthony Fauci, the longtime director of the National Institute of Allergy and Infectious Diseases at the National Institutes of Health, to help devise the architecture and the goals of the program. Dybul was a slightly built, high-energy physician who had developed finely tuned tactical, political, and diplomatic skills to help sustain an awkward marriage of liberal Democrats and conservative Christian Republicans in the AIDS effort. These strange bedfellows included a sizable number of Christian leaders around the country who worked in both publicly and privately funded programs in Africa. Dybul, in particular, urged me to look at the practices of some of the tens of thousands of small projects linked to faith-based missions, school projects, and nongovernmental organizations for orphans in Africa. The senior U.S. officials, including some of the unsung leaders of the AIDS fight in U.S. embassies across Africa, such as Warren "Buck" Buckingham in Kenya and Gray Handley in South Africa, said that while African countries generally had a good idea about the activities of large NGOs, such as Save the Children, and multilateral organizations, such as UNICEF, the legions of small groups were simply too many to track. These officials and host government leaders in many cases had no idea of the scope or impact of the private missions. In some countries, scores of Americans were arriving on airplanes each week to do volunteer work. For African government officials seeking a broad understanding of how to meet the needs of children in their countries, this knowledge gap was frustrating. A patchwork faith-based quilt of organizations was invisible to government officials, even as the groups' work was palpably affecting the lives of countless African citizens. This lack of oversight appeared to be getting more widespread, not less.

Everywhere I traveled in Africa while on reporting trips for the *Globe*, I heard from U.S. embassy officials that the number of people working on projects to help children was rapidly increasing. Some estimated it had doubled every year starting early in the first decade of the twenty-first century.

The U.S. Agency for International Development (USAID) was created in 1961, and since then, polls have indicated a widespread belief among Americans that foreign aid constitutes 20 to 25 percent of the federal budget. A majority of people, even those in the development field, believe that the U.S. government is the single largest foreign aid donor in the world. Both beliefs are far off the mark. U.S. foreign assistance accounts for about 1 percent of the federal budget. And the biggest donors are not U.S. government organizations but private American citizens who, according to studies starting in 2004, give three to four times as much as the federal government. Some of the biggest givers are U.S. faith-based groups.

In 2006, the Center for Global Prosperity at the Hudson Institute released a report that said in 2004, U.S. private donors gave at least $71.2 billion in overseas charity. Compare that to $21.3 billion from the U.S. government, which included funding programs by the State Department, USAID, and many other agencies and departments. Of the private donations, an estimated $47 billion was in remittances from Americans to families or friends overseas, $9.7 billion was nongovernmental organizations' spending, and $4.5 billion was given by faith-based groups.

Five years later, the Hudson Institute's annual report on charitable giving found that in 2009, private donations had grown to $128 billion, compared to $28.8 billion in public overseas assistance. Of the private donations, roughly $90 billion was in remittances. Faith-based groups contributed $7.2 billion, a 62 percent increase.

Jeremiah Norris, a senior fellow and director of the Center for Science in Public Policy at the Hudson Institute, helped oversee the study and said that faith-based giving in particular was probably seriously underreported in the survey. Faith-based groups do not have to disclose their donations to the Internal Revenue Service, making all estimates likely to be far under the actual amount given. "That is the tip of the iceberg in faith-based giving," he told me. "Religious organizations now probably do more than USAID does in Africa." In 2009, USAID's $16.6 billion budget was whittled down to under $9 billion in its development programs for Africa, Asia, and Latin America, after reducing funds designated to organizations such as the World Bank and the Global Fund to Fight AIDS, Tuberculosis and Malaria, Norris said. Of that amount, USAID's total funding for global health programs in 2009 was $5.27 billion; about $680 million went to child survival and maternal health programs.

Using information gathered by Emory University, the Hudson Institute report calculated that U.S. churches in 2009 gave $1.7 billion to African projects. Again, Norris said, that number was much lower than the actual amount, calling it a "fraction" of the total giving. Norris said the figure didn't include the billions of dollars spent by churches in Africa to run hospitals, health clinics, and tiny health posts. In some countries, Christian groups, most notably the Catholic Church, provide 50 percent or more of all health services.

Norris said he wasn't surprised by the depth of support from U.S. faith-based groups. "Religious groups pass what we call a 'market test': They continue to be supported by groups at home because they do something that has measureable impact. They also have been out there way before USAID."

Oprah Winfrey and David Nixon, then, were cousins in this vast, private tsunami of giving. On the surface, they didn't seem to have much in common: one a glamorous African American celebrity known worldwide by her first name, the other a balding white American whose life outside Charlotte, North Carolina, did not have a high quotient of glamour. But both shared an inner drive to look beyond their busy lives; seeing a great need in the growing ranks of orphans in Africa, they were driven to do something about it.

Nixon's faith-inspired motivation was shared by many in the swelling ranks of donors Norris had described. It was a modern-day version of a long line of European and North American missionaries, predecessors who had left behind mixed results. Some would say they left a positive legacy by setting up health and education systems in Africa. But many of the missionaries from the eighteenth, nineteenth, and early twentieth centuries were closely tied to colonialists, and most historians believe that the colonialists and the clergy had strong reasons to support each other.

The colonialists, who robbed the Africans of their independence, allowed the missionaries a new frontier in which to convert Africans to Christianity. Quoting Bible passages such as "love your neighbor as you love yourself" and "blessed are the humble for the kingdom of God is theirs," the missionaries used religion as a means of encouraging passivity among Africans.

Missionaries in Africa can be traced back to the 1500s along the east coast of Africa, when they joined Portuguese colonizers; priests came to serve as chaplains to the Portuguese garrisons, but later Jesuit and Dominican monks traveled inland to seek converts. At that time, the Roman Catholic Church and the main Protestant denominations in Europe did not oppose the slave trade, and some Christian leaders argued that the Bible supported it. But by the late eighteenth and early nineteenth centuries, many Christians had joined the abolitionist movement, and missionaries traveled to Africa to protest the slave trade; some helped set up a colony of expatriated American slaves in West Africa that later became the independent nation of Liberia. Over a period of half a century, the American Colonization Society sent more than 13,000 freed African Americans to Africa as an alternative to freedom in the United States. However, the motives of the American Colonization Society were by no means pure: many of its members were openly racist and some supported sending slaves to Africa because of fears that blacks working for low wages in America would take away jobs from whites.

In Africa, converting Africans to Christianity began to take off during the late 1800s. During a period of about eighty years, tens of thousands of missionaries arrived, and Christianity spread like wildfire. At the beginning of the twentieth century, the number of Christians in Africa was estimated at 9 million. At the end of the first decade of the twenty-first century, Africa had an estimated 450 million Christians in a population nearing 1 billion. In recent decades, this massive flocking to Christianity has been fueled in large part by evangelicals, rather than by Catholics and mainstream Protestants. A 2006 Pew Forum on Religion and Public Life study found that 147 million African Christians identified themselves as evangelical Christians, which included Pentecostals and Charismatics.

In the early years of the twenty-first century, Africa had by far the fastest growing and most diverse group of Christians in the world. In the Roman Catholic Church, the power of Africa's millions grew so great that a Nigerian cardinal, Francis Arinze, was on the shortlist to succeed Pope Jean Paul II in 2005. Nigeria at the time had 76 million Christians, 48 percent of its population, which meant that it was number 6 in the world in terms of its Christian population. In 2010, the number of baptized Catholics in Nigeria alone was estimated at more than 19 million. Right behind Nigeria was the Democratic Republic of Congo, with 68 million Christians. Both were ahead of Italy, which was at number 9 with 55 million Christians. The United States, by comparison, had a higher percentage of Christians than the continent of Africa, 78 percent of the population, and it led the world in the number of Christians, 243 million.

As for the missionaries' secondary goal of educating African children, the results were at times impressive, as faith-based schools became well established throughout the continent and were often an integral part of a country's educational system. Yet the system of education in many African countries remains a dismal failure, from primary school to universities. In 2007, approximately 46 million African children had never attended school at all. Some estimated that those children plus the number of dropouts meant that roughly 43 percent of all the school-age children in Africa were not in school. These estimations deepened many Americans' feeling that Africa was a hopeless continent. (Statistics that clumped all of Africa together often had this effect; for instance, even if a high number of Africa's fifty-three countries showed economic improvement, a cluster of poorly performing nations would drag down trend lines for all.)

The problems have touched Americans for decades. Starting from the early missionaries and continuing until today, tens of thousands of Americans have regularly given small and large amounts of money to groups working in Africa, answering pleas from a variety of organizations to save an African child. Actress Sally Struthers was one of the most famous for making these pleas, showing up in TV spots asking each American to donate a nickel a day to save the life of an African child dying of famine. Many charities, including Save the Children and Plan USA, used a version of this type of plea, and these organizations are now familiar to most Americans. Some of these modes of giving promised that the donor would have a personal relationship with the sponsored child, often via an ongoing exchange of letters. In the 2002 movie *About Schmidt*, a retired insurance executive in Omaha, Nebraska, played by Jack Nicholson, writes almost weekly to Ndugu, a child he sponsored for twenty-two dollars a month. Nicholson's character slowly reveals more and more about his personal life. It was a striking parable of the complicated emotions these incentives tap into, reflecting the great humanitarian impulses of American givers and their psychological need to offer help to some of the most economically vulnerable people on earth.

In the 1980s and 1990s, the attention Americans paid to Africa's children increased dramatically. The largest reason was AIDS. The pandemic, thought to have originated in Africa in the 1920s or 1930s but first identified in the United States in 1981, made the deepest inroads in sub-Saharan Africa. It circulated largely through heterosexual sex, and its victims were those in their teens, twenties, thirties, and forties. This population included many parents and the workers who were the most productive members of society. Soon after 2000, groups such as UNICEF and the Joint United Nations Programme on HIV/AIDS (UNAIDS) warned of an AIDS orphan crisis spiraling out of control; more than a million children were projected to lose one or both parents to the disease every year for at least the next decade. Some American national security officials, including those at the Central Intelligence Agency's leading think tank, the National Intelligence Council, warned that the widespread deaths of young adults could destabilize militaries and governments. These accounts and others warned that if the pandemic did not abate, and if those already infected continued to die, societies would consist largely of the very young and the very old. Furthering that analysis, some talked about the possibility of a developing underclass of feral children—homeless wanderers, thieves, and illiterate and lawless bands who would become a threat to the security of nations. I always disliked the term *feral children.* It was so demeaning, and I wondered how true it was. I had heard stories of African children wandering from village to village, begging for or stealing food, and of their moving to the cities of Africa and living an Oliver Twist existence. In many cities, ranging from the vast metropolis of Lagos, Nigeria, to the smaller city of Kisumu, Kenya, I did find scores of children fending for themselves, living on the extreme edges of society. Some fell into prostitution; others sold individual pieces of gum or single cigarettes to survive.

But when I tried to verify these anecdotal accounts of bands of children roaming in rural parts of Africa, I couldn't. The stories were likely true, but they were also likely extreme examples of what was happening in countries hard hit by AIDS. Most extended families and most communities took care of these orphans. It was part of their DNA. But these warnings of feral children, along with the corresponding rise of child soldiers in several African countries—tens of thousands fought in the horrific conflicts in Sierra Leone, Liberia, Democratic Republic of Congo, and Uganda, among others, over the past two decades—had the intended effects of sending shivers down the spines of the world's policymakers and capturing the attention of the world's media.

Yet in the early years of the twenty-first century, rich governments had not made much of a commitment to helping orphans in Africa. The overriding perspective, at least in Washington during the last part of the Clinton administration and at the beginning of the Bush administration, was that the problem was too big. They believed the AIDS crisis was out of control and that there was no way to fight AIDS because the drugs cost too much and were too difficult to get to Africans on a large scale. In an interview in June of 2001, Andrew Natsios, who had just been appointed administrator of the U.S. Agency for International Development, told me that a wide-scale distribution of antiretroviral drugs to Africans was a nonstarter because the infrastructure was so bad and because Africans didn't "know how to tell time."

My story in the *Globe* that morning immediately drew a storm of protest from advocates. Some appeared outside USAID's headquarters in Washington wearing giant clock placards and urging Natsios to resign. The next day Natsios repeated his comments before the House Committee on International Relations. In many parts of Africa, he told lawmakers, "people do not know what watches or clocks are. They do not use Western means to tell time. They use the sun. These drugs have to be administered in certain sequences, at certain times during the day. You say, take it at ten o'clock, they say, what do you mean, ten o'clock?"

People in the hearing room gasped. Despite the calls for Natsios's resignation, he survived the turmoil. He wasn't alone in his ill-informed thinking at the time, but new combination medicines meant that those with AIDS had to take fewer pills and could simply swallow them with meals or at the beginning and end of the day. Even though no one doubted the need to do something to stop AIDS, which caused the number of African orphans to soar rapidly (officials estimated roughly 15 million children under the age of eighteen had lost one or both parents to AIDS, and that number could double in a decade), the official response was tepid. Political will didn't exist. There seemed to be too many reasons why powerful governments couldn't attack the problem in Africa and around the world: lack of money, lack of infrastructure, and (if you listened to Natsios) even a lack of wristwatches.

Then it all changed in Washington, with the help of an unlikely catalyst: President Bush, who had previously been dismissive of the effectiveness of foreign aid. In 2003, in a State of the Union address dominated by his making the case for war against Iraq, Bush announced that he would launch a major initiative to fight HIV/AIDS. Congress later approved the President's Emergency Plan for AIDS Relief (PEPFAR), a plan that in its first five years spent more than $19 billion to fight AIDS in fifteen countries, twelve of them in Africa. It would be the most money ever spent by a government to fight a single disease.

Just before the inception of PEPFAR, the Global Fund to Fight AIDS, Tuberculosis, and Malaria was formed in Geneva, and the U.S. government and other nations began contributing to its efforts. That start, which occurred at the very same time that David Nixon was beginning his journey in Malawi, triggered more and more public funding. In 2011, more than 4 million people with AIDS in the developing world were able to take antiretroviral drugs because of the support of PEPFAR, the Global Fund, and host-country governments. It was a historic achievement, and a large share of the credit could go to a Republican administration. By 2009, according to the Kaiser Family Foundation, the United States was contributing 58 percent of all public global funding to fight HIV and AIDS.

Some American religious leaders and members of Congress influenced by the Christian Right formed a united front to push for AIDS prevention funding that emphasized abstinence. While the bulk of PEPFAR's funding was geared toward treatment (55 percent), palliative care (15 percent), and aid to orphans and vulnerable children (10 percent), the other 20 percent of the money was targeted for prevention. Of that 20 percent, one-third was earmarked for abstinence programs, a longtime favorite of the Christian Right. This 6.66 percent of the PEPFAR budget became a lightning rod for dissent by both liberal commentators and many public health experts, who argued that the administration and Congress could show no evidence that abstinence programs had reduced the incidence rate of HIV. But several PEPFAR officials responded that abstinence teaching could have some role in fighting HIV if national and tribal leaders preached it and that advocates fighting AIDS should do all they could to reduce risky sexual behavior and delay the age of sexual debut for young people. Privately, senior administration officials told me that even if the abstinence policy could not be proven to slow the spread of HIV, including it in PEPFAR's strategy had an indisputable positive political consequence: it helped to create broad-based, bipartisan support, forming a coalition of liberal Democrats and conservative Republicans that was unheard-of on almost any issue, let alone global health. That broad support meant in general that funding requests sailed through Congress. AIDS, suddenly, was being fought by billions of public U.S. dollars, supported by conservatives such as Jesse Helms and liberals such as Edward Kennedy.

This was the African aid landscape that a new generation of missionaries was entering. In large part, they did not go to Africa with the same goals as their predecessors; proselytizing, for many, was not their top priority. Now, going to Africa was more about following Christian values by helping some of the most vulnerable people on earth. Outside Washington's Beltway, disconnected from the politics of AIDS and abstinence on Capitol Hill, hundreds and hundreds of American churches large and small, in a largely uncoordinated parallel effort, mounted their own unprecedented charitable responses. Megachurches, such as Rick Warren's Saddleback Church and Bishop Charles Blake's West Angeles Church of God, started AIDS programs that at their core emphasized helping African children. U.S. faith-based groups held at least a dozen conferences on AIDS from 2003 to 2007. Word spread rapidly from congregation to congregation. Hundreds, if not thousands, of churches began sending delegations to Africa each year to explore how they could become involved.

And adding momentum to this groundswell, celebrities began to tell the media about the virtues of getting involved. George Clooney campaigned for an end to the violence in the Darfur region of Sudan, and Oprah Winfrey started talking with Mandela in 2000 about how she could help in South Africa; seven years later, she christened her academy. In Malawi, Madonna attracted worldwide attention with her intention to adopt a one-year-old boy who was staying at an orphanage despite having a father. Madonna asked her representatives to set up a charity through which she could quietly help thousands of other children in the small south-central African country, an action that went largely unreported.

Angelina Jolie and Brad Pitt adopted a child from Ethiopia. Jolie gave roughly $1 million to help start an advocacy group in Washington, DC, to advance the interests of African children. "Orphaned children are the world's children," she said at a news conference in Washington in 2007. "We know the price of our indifference. I hope people are inspired to learn more and get involved."

And the Irish rock star Bono turned into a behind-the-scenes politician, knowing just the right touch—or gift—for world leaders he sought out. In a private meeting with Bush, just prior to the announcement of the U.S. global AIDS program, the U.S. president, who had to be cajoled into meeting with Bono, found himself speechless when Bono gave him an old Irish Bible. Bush, one aide told me later, was almost reduced to tears.

Lost in this sudden hubbub of activity and the cascade of targeted messaging from these powerful advocates, faith-based groups, celebrities, and government officials was a simple question: Did any of them know the best ways to help African children?

The question stayed with me throughout my many trips to Africa. It seemed to me that there had to be groups with a good understanding of the best ways to help. But it also seemed that many Americans were arriving in Africa with no idea of how to aid children in a foreign land. What was happening when they ventured into cities or rural villages? Why did so many want to build orphanages? I wanted to find out whether their good intentions were being translated into actions that the beneficiaries themselves found helpful. Were they in fact doing good?

Chapter 4

An Education in Malawi

David Nixon was like many Americans who go to Africa to help orphans. He didn't have a concrete plan, but he had an unshakable determination to do something for the vulnerable children. He had some general ideas and was confident that he could raise money back home to make this desire a reality. Above all, Nixon believed, like many Americans who went to Africa on faith-based missions, that he was doing the work that God had set out for him, and that whatever he did would be guided by the Lord. God's will will be done, he thought. That meant that while he was making plans to go forward, he was always asking for God's direction. Prayer, whether in internal whisperings or end-of-day call-outs to God, felt like a surrender of himself to the Lord. Afterward, he felt blessed, always, even if trouble clung to him like a T-shirt in a soaking afternoon rain. For several years, starting from the moment he landed in Africa, he was on a journey directed by his faith in God. It began with the seed of an idea to build an orphanage in Africa; he planted that seed and then watched as many things went wrong: roadblocks, setbacks, threats, dangers. This was the education of David Nixon. He would learn as he went, painful as it almost always was. And he would emerge having learned more than he ever could have imagined. He did have one surety: God was showing him the way. Nixon fervently believed he was just an instrument in his Maker's hands, and even though trouble would cause him to cry out as Job cried out to God, he would march on. Some called him stubborn. He called himself a believer.

At the end of his first day in Malawi, Nixon waited for the other travelers from North Carolina—John O. Danford, his wife, and their young companion—at the airport. Nixon and his two buddies from Emmanuel Baptist could barely wait to tell them of their experiences so far.

But the excitement soon faded. They picked up the other travelers and drove from the airport to their guesthouse, and then the six of them sat together in a small living room around a coffee table and started to discuss their plans for the next several days. Nixon and his two friends first told the others about their decision to give money to the local pastors to buy food for their communities. The three men were still elated because it seemed to them that they had likely saved many lives by their decisive action. But Danford didn't see it that way. From across the coffee table, Nixon watched his smile disappear and his eyes narrow. Danford told them that this was not the way he wanted to do things, and that they were out of line. This trip, he reminded them, was his to direct; the newcomers from Monroe were not to dictate and influence. He was the one with experience in working in Malawi, not them.

Danford reminded them that his philosophy in helping out people in Malawi did not include making snap decisions. After all, he had first traveled to Malawi some seventeen years before, in 1985, and he had a track record that they lacked. "I've been here a long time, and I know the way it works," he said. "The long term is our commitment, not to go fast and furious. It is about relationships, and working with people, arm in arm."

Nixon and his friends still felt they had done the right thing. After all, they told Danford, wasn't the purpose of coming to Malawi to save lives? And hadn't they done just that?

While showing respect to Danford, Nixon disagreed with Danford's description of the mission. Nixon said that all had agreed they would work toward a common goal. The distinction, Nixon said, was important. If the three church members from Monroe wanted to explore something that they felt strongly about, they should be free to do so.

Danford relented somewhat. He agreed that he would consider Nixon's perspective as the group moved forward. What remained unspoken was that Nixon had helped underwrite the cost of Danford's trip to Africa. That made him a donor, and while he wasn't going to use that to try to get his way, Nixon wasn't going to blindly follow Danford if he disagreed with him.

Baucom and Tarlton watched from the sidelines. Tarlton wanted to smooth things over, so he spoke up a few times during the conversation to try to make things right. Baucom just listened. He viewed them as the Three Musketeers, with Nixon as their leader. In Baucom's view, Danford seemed to be upset that the first-timers were running ahead without him, and he wanted to regain control.

But amid the tension, Baucom saw a side of Nixon he hadn't fully appreciated before: he was a diplomat. Nixon, he knew, wanted to move at a hundred miles per hour on a project that would help children, but Baucom could see that Nixon realized he couldn't do it alone—he needed cooperation from Danford, African preachers connected to Danford, and Tarlton and himself. Baucom watched Nixon attempt to win the group's support. Still, Baucom wasn't optimistic that this partnership with Danford would work. Nixon, like Tarlton and himself, was in a bit of a hurry to get things done, and Danford seemed in no hurry. He seemed most interested in setting up times to preach, not in working on a project that would benefit orphans in one of the local ministries.

On the second day after Danford's arrival, the six of them drove in a large van to a village called Chakwindima, named after the local chief, about an hour southeast of Lilongwe. Prior to his arrival in Malawi, Danford had heard from some of his pastor friends that one group in Chakwindima was interested in starting an orphan-care center, and he wanted the Americans to meet them and hear more about their plans.

When they got out of the van, a group of Malawians began to walk toward them, singing. It was here that Nixon vowed to himself that he would do something on this land for children. Tears ran down his cheeks.

As the two groups came together and the Malawians finished their songs of praise for the Lord, the local church leaders told the Americans that they had talked to the chief about getting land in Chakwindima for a project for children. They told Nixon and the others that the chief had given his verbal approval.

Nixon took particular notice of one of the Malawians: a rail-thin local preacher named Jacques Jackson who spoke movingly to the American group in his welcome, thanking them and praising the Lord for their visit. Jackson, with his chiseled cheekbones, his beautiful wife, Mary, and their adorable young daughter charmed the group from Monroe. Jackson, who had converted to Christianity from Islam several years before, had grown up in extreme poverty in a remote village in Malawi, one of sixteen children of a father who fished for a living. He had risen out of the village through education, achieving a teacher's certificate from a Malawi college, and was serving as a headmaster of a local government school. He had also taken several months of courses at a Billy Graham–sponsored school of ministry. Through these experiences, he had developed leadership qualities, and he started to harbor dreams of growing his own congregation and doing something to help the increasing number of orphans in the villages around him. He could see the need every morning when he taught in the government school. More and more children had lost one or both parents and they plainly suffered because of it. They missed the love from their mothers and fathers, the stability in their family, and they saw their opportunities shrink because of new financial realities. It meant that their extended families had no money for their schooling and that sometimes meals were scarce.

Jackson knew the Americans were coming. He had learned from his briefings with pastors connected to Danford that the Americans wanted to support a project that would help children. So their arrival, he believed, could be a pivotal moment in his life.

When the singing ended, Jackson explained to the Americans that they were building a simple structure that would serve as their church. Jackson said that he had already talked to the village chief about constructing some type of a center for orphans, and the chief had given him a large plot of land in the village to use for both the church and as a place for children to gather and possibly live. At the site, the visitors prayed and rejoiced in the Lord, and they experienced something more grounded: the making of bricks that would be used for the foundation of the church.

The Malawians showed the group how they made the bricks. At first, the Americans simply stood on the sidelines watching as the Malawians used wooden molds to make bricks out of water, river sand, and mud. The bricks were stacked and heated under a fire until they solidified. Nixon and Tarlton eventually jumped into the ditches and made bricks side by side with the Malawians.

This was a tried-and-true approach to making volunteers feel invested in a project: having them get their hands dirty by building or renovating something. Indeed, the Monroe visitors felt exhilarated. They could see the tangible benefits of making bricks and laying them: they were helping to build the foundation for a church, and perhaps they would be involved with this same group to build a center for the children.

Danford, aware of Nixon's construction background, asked Nixon to help sketch out the church building. On a pad of paper at the site, Nixon made a rough outline of a house of worship. He drew a basic rectangular structure with windows and a door and made a list of materials they would need. He talked with Tarlton and Baucom, and the three men decided that buying supplies for the group would be a great way to spend the $500 given to them by the Emmanuel Baptist church leaders. Nixon, mindful of Danford's earlier objections in directly funding projects in Malawi, asked Danford if he thought it would be okay for them to use the money in this way. Danford gave his blessing.

The Americans drove into town and purchased wood and tools for digging and making bricks: shovels, pickaxes, and wheelbarrows. Over the next several days, the group laid out the base of the building, and Nixon instructed the Malawians to dig deep trenches for its footings. The Americans handed out the newly bought tools, but the Malawians, while grateful, quickly discarded the shovels and pickaxes and continued using handcrafted hoes that were each made out of the base of a tree: a trimmed root ball was the handle, and it was attached to a flat piece of steel. The wheelbarrows were the only items that came in handy. The Malawians clearly had their own way of doing things and their own tools that worked perfectly well, which the Americans finally realized, chagrined that their seemingly more advanced tools really weren't an improvement in this village. They gained an appreciation for the skills of the local builders.

Nixon, an experienced carpenter, marveled at the group. They worked harder than any crew he had seen back home. It was difficult digging the trenches, but the group kept at it with what Nixon called their Malawian hoes. Baucom couldn't understand why people with such strong construction skills lived in round mud huts with fire pits in the middle for cooking. He was also bemused by the ground itself, which seemed immaculate. Women and children, he later learned, were constantly sweeping the ground in order to keep the village clean and their huts less dusty. When he later returned to North Carolina, he would tell friends with a note of incredulity in his voice, "They swept the ground clean!"

During these intense days in Malawi, Nixon, Baucom, and Tarlton felt they were constantly learning. They stayed in cramped quarters—in a little apartment behind the house of the Malawian businessman Mr. Maliro, who was a good friend of Danford. Their beds were draped by mosquito nets, as malaria was an ever-present threat in Malawi, and they were appropriately concerned about it at night when the disease-transmitting female *Anopheles* mosquito was out. On that first night, Tarlton heard a mosquito buzzing in his ear. He sprang up and shone his flashlight around the net, finding two things: the mosquito and a hole large enough for many more mosquitoes to enter. He killed the mosquito and pulled his sheet up around his ears until morning.

They were extremely careful about what they ate. Back home, numerous people had told them about how they had gotten sick while traveling overseas. And so the three stuck to the same diet day after day: lots of canned food and crackers that they bought in a local store. One frequent meal was potted meat, a spreadable mix of beef, pork, chicken, and turkey in a can; the men referred to it as pâté.

Tarlton had brought along a couple of bags of candy to hand out to children. During the first visit to Chakwindima, during a break in the singing and praying, Tarlton, with Nixon and Baucom watching from the sidelines, pulled out one bag of candy and started calling the children. Within a minute, dozens of kids were running toward him. He tried to calm them down and line them up, but they tugged at his clothes, calling excitedly for the *azungu* to give them a piece of candy. It became chaotic, and Tarlton, just to give himself some room, threw handfuls of candy away from them. He realized immediately that he had made a mistake. Many of the older children trampled the smallest ones to get a piece, and the commotion only drew more children to the swarm around him. They pulled at his pants and shirt, and he gave the candy out as fast as he could, feeling awful that the larger kids were pushing aside the smallest. All of them learned something at that moment, and it was about much more than just candy. It was about knowing what was appropriate and inappropriate in a foreign setting. Tarlton thought he was being generous by bringing candy, but he left knowing that he had created a stampede that had hurt some of the smaller children. The experience made them realize that they knew a lot less than they thought they did, and perhaps they should ask local people first before doing or saying something in public that could do more harm than good.

After ten days in Malawi, Tarlton and Baucom flew home to North Carolina. Nixon stayed another two weeks, shooting more videos and meeting almost daily with Jackson. Nixon made sketches for other buildings, and, wary of relying on only the chief's verbal agreement to allow them to use the land for an orphanage, he strongly encouraged Jackson to get the chief to sign a legal document. They made some key overarching decisions. Nixon believed that the concept of an orphan-care center needed to be defined more clearly. He suggested that they start an orphanage, and Jackson agreed. In the initial phase of the project, Nixon tasked Jackson with traveling to surrounding villages and finding children who had lost their parents. Jackson would compile that information and send it to Nixon, who would start fund-raising in the United States.

Nixon was unlike any person Jackson had ever known; he was even quite different from the few foreigners Jackson had met before. Nixon was full of energy. He frenetically moved from one task to the other, and he worked longer than anyone else in the village. Nixon represented a new hope for Jackson and his family, as well as the many others who might be employed by him. It was easy to look at Nixon as a rich white American, as someone Jackson should cater to because he might personally reap benefits. But Jackson looked at Nixon as someone who could help him fulfill a dream to help many children in need around him. Jackson couldn't be completely certain, though; he wasn't sure whether he could trust this boundlessly energetic American. Would he come back? Would he stick to this project or move on to a new one first? Jackson had no firsthand experience working for a white foreigner before, and some of his friends warned him that a white foreigner wasn't to be trusted. He had to earn that trust, they told Jackson. So far, though, in these first days, Jackson liked Nixon. And he liked the fact that Nixon seemed to genuinely need him.

Nixon and Jackson talked about starting more serious construction later in the year if they had the funding. When Nixon left, he told Jackson that he hoped to be back soon— with enough funds to build an orphanage.

On the flight home to the United States, Danford and Nixon had a stopover for several hours at the O. R. Tambo International Airport in Johannesburg, South Africa.

Along with Danford's wife and her young companion, Nixon and Danford sat down at a food court in the airport. After they'd all said the blessing over their food, Danford's wife and her companion moved to another table so the two men could talk privately.

The two had reached an uneasy détente in Malawi. Danford realized that he could push Nixon only so far, and Nixon knew he could get only so much cooperation out of Danford. Danford had brought in Nixon for a specific project and had introduced him to the local preachers. But Nixon brought energy and, he believed, he'd soon be able to raise money for the projects. Nixon had been anticipating this conversation for days while in Malawi. He dearly wanted to make a break from Danford and work alone on this project because he didn't think the two could work together. It wasn't just Danford's slow pace; it was also his relationship with the local Malawian pastors, including Jackson and several other ministers whom Danford had known for years. Several of the pastors had told Nixon that they felt Danford treated them as inferior, almost like children. Were they being honest? Were they trying to win additional support from Nixon? Nixon couldn't be totally certain. But he had sensed a tension between Danford and the pastors. He knew that Danford had to show authority as the leader of the projects, but Nixon believed he himself would have handled things differently if he were in charge. As Danford eyed him suspiciously across the table, Nixon told him he wanted to go ahead with the orphans project and would be raising money and returning to Malawi in the near future. He said he wanted to move independently. Nixon sensed that Danford was in a difficult position, as he lacked access to major funding for the project, but he still didn't want to let go of it. Danford told Nixon that it was okay with him if Nixon moved ahead. Danford said that anything Nixon could do to help people in that village, especially the children, would be a blessing. To Nixon, that sounded as if Danford understood they would no longer work together. He would later find out that this was not the older man's understanding, but by then it would be too late: Nixon had found his calling and he was going to run with it.

▲ ▲ ▲ ▲

Once in North Carolina again, the three men from Emmanuel Baptist began planning their next steps. Their first job was to report back to their pastor and church. Nixon edited his video into a twenty-minute production, a rough cut that showed the power of the moment, the welcoming of Malawians, and the great need of the children. In separate conversations with church members, Nixon and his travel partners described in stark terms how the children lived with almost nothing and how they lacked nutritional food, basic clothing, and any educational opportunities.

Even before they showed the video, the three realized that though people seemed to care about what they had done, their interest wasn't deep or lasting. When Baucom started talking about Africa, he found that people's eyes began drifting away from him, their attitude conveying *Okay, great, I've got to run.* It was hard for Americans to connect to Africa, to children who were starving or who had lost their parents to AIDS. They were so far, far away. The stories were heartbreaking, people told them. And, they said, they were so happy that the three men had gone and done God's work in Africa. What a blessing! But the three knew instinctively that most of those comments were superficial. It wasn't that the people were uncaring. It was that they couldn't comprehend the situation. They hadn't been in their shoes, and they hadn't seen the poverty and suffering for themselves.

So the men descended from the high of connecting with another world that desperately needed their help to being frustrated and more than a little depressed in their familiar lives in North Carolina. They had experienced firsthand the emotional power of being in Africa, a feeling of time suspended, of living in the present. There was so much to drink in there, each scene captivating because it was so *foreign:* the mothers sitting in the shade of giant trees, breastfeeding babies; the red dust rising from the road as they drove into the bush, coating their forearms and faces, and the joy in feeling so gritty; and the swarms of beautiful children running to them whenever they got out of the car in a village, eyes sparkling at them, smiles showing off half-moon rows of white teeth. They felt encouraged to do anything they could for these children. And yet back home in America, they were unable to translate those powerful feelings for their friends and acquaintances. Others didn't truly understand the vast gulf between what Americans had and what Malawians had because it was still too much of an abstract notion. It was as if you had to go to Africa and see the children who had such potential and yet such limited opportunity to realize it before you could feel the urgency of helping them.

They faced an additional problem. Pastor Hildreth and some of the deacons of the church wanted to know how to bring the Gospel to the communities in Malawi. The three travelers tried to explain that the church communities there had less need for teaching and more need for roofs to pray under, and the Emmanuel Baptist hierarchy didn't like that answer. They wanted to convert souls. When they understood that was not the three men's top priority, they grew indifferent. The three men realized they had lost the support of the church leaders. For Baucom especially, this was disillusioning. It was as if the only thing that mattered to the leaders were their preconceived notions of what they should be doing in Africa. No one, he thought, had bothered to really listen to their descriptions of the need they witnessed in Africa.

But some people did engage with the men's experience, especially after watching the video and listening to Nixon onstage. The images, the narration, and Nixon's sometimes thunderous oration drew them in and often caused many in the audience to tear up.

After one such talk and showing of the video at a small church in Unionville, North Carolina, about eight miles north of Monroe, the pastor told the gathering that the church had been saving up for exactly such a mission and suggested turning over the entire account to Nixon. The audience enthusiastically agreed. The amount was $18,000. Other churches also pitched in, and in three months, Nixon had collected $39,000. The number astounded him.

A major disappointment awaited Nixon at Emmanuel Baptist though. After Nixon gave a rousing talk and showed the video to a few hundred people, Hildreth stood to thank Nixon and praised him for the project he had begun under church auspices. He then instructed his ushers to start a collection and urged parishioners to give generously. Nixon could see people in the church wiping their eyes and blowing their noses, writing out checks, and digging into their wallets and pocketbooks. The ushers returned with baskets overflowing with money. Hildreth then asked his congregation for a special second collection for the Malawi mission. Nixon sat dumbfounded. Hadn't Hildreth just asked people to give to his mission a few moments before? He watched again as the baskets passed down the rows, with people putting in far less money and checks this time. Afterward, several people in the audience came up to Nixon to apologize, saying they had given all they had in the first collection, which they assumed would go to the children in Malawi. They had nothing left to give, they said.

Nixon, accompanied by Baucom, sought out Hildreth after the service and told him that he and others in the audience thought the first collection was for the Malawi mission. Hildreth said they were mistaken—he said he clearly had intended the money to go the church. Nixon told his pastor that he respectfully disagreed. Standing next to Nixon, Baucom silently agreed with Nixon. The whole thing was so confusing to Baucom. Nixon would later reason that Pastor Hildreth had a church to look after, and his congregation in Monroe had to be his top priority. Baucom, though, began to look differently at the inner circles of power in the church. As he saw it, everyone on earth was human and made errors, and his pastor was just like everyone else, prone to bad judgments from time to time. It couldn't be helped, he thought. But the episode left a bad taste in the mouths of all three men. Over the next several months, all would leave Emmanuel Baptist. The experience didn't shake their faith, but it did alter their views of the management of the church.

It was painful to feel that his church had deceived him, but Nixon's desire to get something done in Malawi was unflagging. With the donations coming in, he made plans to return three months after his first trip. He had stayed in close touch with Jackson, who was supervising the orphanage project there. He also had come up with a name for his project. Kamphambe, the village chief, had said that he would let the group use the land for the orphans' project on one condition: its official designation had to include the name Nlira-Wanga. The chief said that the land belonged to a large family that had once lived on the land. Over the generations, some members had moved away, and some had died in a famine, and now no one was left. In the Chichewa language, *nlira-wanga* means "I am crying for my own." Nixon agreed to the chief's request, but he struggled with it. *How can I use this name and still make Americans understand what the project is about?* he thought. One night that fall as he lay awake in his bed, the answer came to him—he would use an acronym: NOAH, which stood for Nlira-Wanga Orphan Aid Homes. For Nixon, Noah and his ark represented the possibility of saving a world that was dying and corrupt. In October of 2002, Nixon took his second trip to Malawi. Jackson had done a thorough survey that identified more than a hundred orphans who could move into the orphanage. They hired 120 men to build the houses for the children, and Nixon decided to purchase twenty beds and mattresses to get started. In the village, Kamphambe laughed when Nixon told him the name of the project.

"You are like Moses, and you are like Noah too," Kamphambe said. "God told Noah to build an ark and everyone laughed at him." The same was true in the village, the chief said: no one there believed that the American would come back, live up to his word, and build an orphanage. Nixon said he appreciated the support, but he was still wary of the chief.

In earlier discussions, Jackson had warned Nixon that the chief would likely want something in return for his gift of allowing the project to build on the land, which belonged to the community but, according to local practice, was under the chief's control. Nixon was thankful for Jackson's insight into the culture and politics of the village, as he had no idea of what cues he should look for. In fact, Nixon realized, he was already depending quite a bit on Jackson, whom he had met only a few months earlier. He gave this some thought. He was concerned that he was putting so much trust in someone he barely knew. This wouldn't be the approach of John Danford, who believed in going slowly and testing his local contacts over time for trustworthiness. But the Danford way, Nixon thought, wouldn't work with what he wanted to do: seize the moment and help children in Africa now, rather than years from now. Still, Nixon realized he needed to broaden his perspective and seek guidance from others who were working on aid projects in Malawi. He was being drawn into a world he knew little about, and he needed to find guides whom he could trust.

In Lilongwe, Nixon began to reach out to various nongovernmental organizations, including faith-based groups that consisted of a mix of Malawians and expats. This was the beginning of his education of what to do and what not to do in Africa. In particular, he sought the advice of a faith-based umbrella group called the Network of Organizations for Vulnerable and Orphaned Children, or NOVOC. The leaders of the organization had extensive experience in development and in orphan-related issues. They advised Nixon to get his project off the ground with the construction of a few buildings before approaching Malawian officials to ask for the government's approval to educate and house the children. Only then would the officials take him seriously.

He decided to follow NOVOC's guidance. He would go ahead and build a couple of structures and show the Malawi government that he was serious about his project, and then he would approach the government for permission to run an orphanage. Everything seemed to be in alignment. After staying in Malawi for about a month, Nixon returned to North Carolina and continued to send the money he raised. By the end of 2002, he had also donated $14,000 of his own money to the cause. Because he was investing so much time and energy in the project, he had less time for his construction business in North Carolina and the start-up software company that he had begun with Tarlton. It didn't bother him much. He was too excited about what he had initiated in Malawi.

In July of 2003, Nixon made his third trip to Malawi. His project now consisted of four buildings, an outhouse, and a roster of children ready to be enrolled in his orphanage. He had one overriding goal on this trip: to receive formal approval from the government of Malawi to open an orphanage. He and Jackson set up an appointment to see Malawi's chief child protection officer, Penston S. Kilembe.

In Kilembe's office, Nixon introduced himself, Jackson, and another local pastor named Moses Kachala who worked with Jackson. Kilembe led them over to a sitting area that had two couches facing each other, and Nixon thanked him for taking the time to see them.

Nixon laid out what he and Jackson had accomplished so far. Showing pictures of the property to Kilembe, he told the story of how he had overseen the construction of four buildings and an outhouse on five acres of land donated by a local chief. Some of the buildings would be sleeping quarters for orphans, he said, while others would serve as classrooms. His plan was to open the orphanage sometime during the next several months.

Nixon was just getting warmed up. He felt so proud of what he had accomplished, and he was eager to share his story. But Kilembe cut him off.

"Stop right there," he said kindly. In an even tone, he said, "I will absolutely not give you permission to build a residential orphanage. That will never happen."

Nixon sat stunned. He didn't quite comprehend what Kilembe had said. He felt his face grow warm.

"We do not want orphanages here," Kilembe said to Nixon and the others. "What I want you to do is build a community-based project. I want you to reach out to the surrounding community. I want you to educate the local people and help the local people find the resources they need to take care of these kids."

Nixon felt himself become angry, livid even. *Who is this Penston Kilembe? Is he one of those corrupt African politicians I keep hearing about? What does he really want? What is it going to take to get the government to agree to my orphanage?*

Nixon's face tightened, and he knew that Kilembe would be able to read the anger in his eyes. The American tried to defend his choice, stumbling to find the right words. He said the local church wanted it, pointing to Jackson sitting next to him. He jabbered some more. "There are so many children without parents, kids who have no one to help them," he pleaded.

No, Kilembe said gently. He told Nixon that the best option wasn't to take the children away from their extended families, but to keep them in those families, keep them in their communities, and educate them so that they could build lives of their own.

Nixon wanted to argue some more, but he refrained. He looked at Jackson, who was staring at his feet. He was on his own here. He took a breath and thought for a moment. Maybe he needed to take a step back and regroup, think this over. *And maybe,* he thought, *this is the Lord's will. Maybe God is telling me to hold my tongue.*

"I want you to go home and think about this, and come back and see me tomorrow after you've thought about it," Kilembe said, again in a calm tone. Nixon and Kilembe were not far apart in age, but Nixon felt that Kilembe was treating him like a subordinate.

Nixon, trying to mask his disappointment, said he would do just that, and he walked out. Following Nixon out of the office, down the stairwell, and into the warm, bright sun, Jackson and Kachala didn't say anything. Jackson, too, was stunned and worried. He wondered if Nixon was going to abandon the project now and if all the hard work that he had overseen would be a waste.

The three men walked to the car. Although they said almost nothing to one another, their minds were racing. As he drove away, Nixon thought that Kilembe wanted Nixon to do his job for him. *He's probably thinking that I'm coming here with deep pockets and unlimited resources,* Nixon thought, *and he's probably thinking he can force me to do his bidding.*

He finally vented his anger. "I can't believe this," he said to Jackson and Kachala. "Why are they doing this? What do you think about what he said?"

Jackson mumbled that he wasn't sure what to think. And that was true; he wasn't sure. He had never been in such a high-level meeting with a government official, but he didn't think Kilembe was looking for a bribe. Kilembe, to him, seemed quite certain of his convictions and adamant in his refusal to allow Nixon to open an orphanage. This was not something that Jackson had anticipated. He quietly agreed with Kilembe's perspective, but he was concerned that Kilembe's words would mean the end of the project. For Jackson, that was a devastating prospect.

Nixon stewed as he drove the two men back to the village of Chakwindima, an hour outside Lilongwe. After dropping them off, Nixon returned to Lilongwe and went to his room in the back of Mr. Maliro's house in Area 25. He prayed and thought about the meeting. The more he prayed, the more he realized that this might not be a bad development. In fact, it could be a positive, even beautiful idea. If he didn't put children in a home, he thought, he wouldn't need an enormous staff to take care of them night and day. Without an orphanage, he would have extra money and free time on nights and weekends to do community development, spread the Gospel, and train people as disciples. He wasn't sure what spreading the Gospel would entail—whether he would start preaching more or whether he would continue to be a messenger through his actions. But suddenly he felt that he had options that didn't exist before. Once again, he felt that he was learning as he went.

The next day, as planned, he returned to Kilembe's office. This time, Kilembe sat behind his desk and Nixon took a chair across from him. After spending an evening in prayer and reflection, Nixon had come to feel that Kilembe had taught him invaluable lessons the day before. He had been looking for partners ever since his first trip to Malawi, more than a year ago. But maybe he needed someone who could set him straight instead, and perhaps he had found that person in Kilembe.

The two men exchanged greetings, and Nixon got right to the point.

"I apologize," Nixon said. "I'm ready to listen to you. What do you want me to do?"

Pleased, Kilembe rattled off a long list. He said Nixon had to talk to community leaders about their needs; talk to people at NOVOC about starting a school; learn about every school in his area so he could determine what unmet needs had to be addressed; and set clear guidelines about who would be admitted to his school and who wouldn't.

Nixon and Jackson did as Kilembe instructed. They started holding meetings with community leaders. They took closer looks at nearby schools and documented overcrowding and lack of supplies for students. And, importantly, they set clear guidelines about who would be eligible to enroll in their school. They knew if they were not careful about setting firm rules and educating local leaders about them, they would face a situation not unlike Tarlton's distribution of candy: a chaotic scene of hundreds and hundreds of students rushing into classrooms on the first day of school. They knew the need was that overwhelming. They decided that the only criterion for a child's eligibility would be that he or she had lost at least one parent, and they would make decisions in consultation with local village leaders. Once those decisions were made, they would be final.

After settling these issues, Nixon boarded a plane heading back to the United States. This trip to Malawi had exhausted him. He had expected that this third trip to Malawi would lead to the opening of an orphanage in a few months. Instead, Kilembe's orders had caused him to stop, rethink, and refocus his energies toward a different project. He agreed completely with the plan to open a small school that would provide morning and noon meals for children, yet even with this new guidance and direction, he needed to get away from Malawi for a bit. If he was going to see his project through to the end, he would have to start paying attention to his personal life and avoid burning out; he would have to stay steadily focused on the long-term viability of the project. So instead of going home to North Carolina and raising funds for the final push to open an orphanage, he started to think it was best to let this project sit for a few months and focus instead on building up his own businesses in North Carolina.

His personal savings had dwindled to almost nothing. He had to spend more time with his partners at the software company, which was working on a program that would make it easier for schools to track student performance. Nixon wasn't about to drop his dreams of helping children in Malawi, but for the next months, NOAH became his second priority. However, he continued to look for opportunities to find new funding for the project, giving talks and showing his video whenever possible. He put Jackson on a small salary, roughly a hundred dollars a month, which was slightly higher than what the government paid him and the amount recommended by NOVOC leaders. They wanted to make sure that an American-run NGO would not offer salaries that were far above the local pay scale.

▲▲▲▲

Jackson, with Nixon's input, built a staff of teachers for the school. Nixon became reengaged with NOAH. He had been able to build his business back up modestly, and that gave him more freedom to devote to the school, and the Malawi project once again became the biggest passion in his life. In 2005, the two opened the school with classes from kindergarten to fourth grade, attracting more than

150 children. The school started well. Teachers were motivated. Students were learning. Class sizes ranged from sixty children in the kindergarten to eight in the highest grade, far fewer students per class than in Malawi's public schools, where many classes were stuffed with eighty to a hundred students. Nonetheless, many students didn't attend public school because their parents or caregivers could not afford even the modest fees for school uniforms, books, and other assorted items. Nixon charged nothing for his school. If it weren't for NOAH, many of the students enrolled would not have been able to attend school at all because their caregivers were so poor. The students received two warm meals a day from the feeding center on the property. Nixon and Jackson were extraordinarily happy that they had succeeded in opening a school to help vulnerable children.

It seemed that things were under control. But soon Nixon learned that this wasn't the case at all.

He had started working with Jackson in 2002, and since then, Kamphambe and Jackson had had several run-ins. The chief had pestered Jackson on several occasions to give jobs to many of his friends in the village. Jackson had always deflected the chief's requests by saying that he had more qualified candidates. But in 2005, while Nixon was in North Carolina, Kamphambe called Jackson into his two-room mud-brick house and insisted that Jackson hire his friends. Jackson said he needed to talk with Nixon.

In a phone call, Nixon and Jackson decided not to go along with the chief's wishes. They already had a full staff, and it included several night watchmen from the village. On the following day, Jackson told Kamphambe of the decision. The chief erupted in anger and said that Jackson was a thief and couldn't be trusted. The chief then made additional demands.

"I would like free use of David Nixon's truck; I want my children at this school; and I should be paid every month," the chief told Jackson. Jackson angrily told the chief that Nixon would not pay him anything and that the chief would receive no special favors. The school, he said, was only for children who had lost their parents, and the land was owned by the community and given by the chief as a donation.

The chief's face tightened. He stood, an indication that the meeting was over.

"You know, don't you, that the only way to kill a snake is to chop off the head," the chief told Jackson. It was a threat against Nixon, Jackson knew. But the threat also extended to him, as Nixon's representative.

Over the next several weeks, while Nixon remained in the United States, the trouble escalated. Thieves conducted a series of nighttime raids on houses belonging to NOAH staff members. One night, machete-wielding men came to Jackson's house looking for him. Jackson saw them and slipped out just seconds before the group arrived.

Someone knocked loudly at the door. Mary, Jackson's wife, asked who was there. A man pushed open the door and shone a flashlight into her eyes. Mary struggled to stop the man from entering, but he pushed her aside. Another man rushed in and grabbed her baby from her arms.

From the doorway, nine-year-old Jackisha Jackson, their eldest child, watched as her mother screamed at the men to return her baby boy. Several men ordered Mary to sit down and demanded to know the whereabouts of her husband. She sat on a well-worn couch in their four-room house, her eyes locked on her baby boy. Mary asked for her baby, but they ignored her. She told the men that Jackson was out and had gone to a nearby community to see a leader there. The men started rifling through stacks of documents and books, and one of them demanded all the school's money. Mary replied that they kept no money in the house. Jackisha retreated to her bedroom. When the men followed the girl, Mary screamed at them to leave her alone. The men ordered Jackisha to go sit with her mother and they started to tear apart the small house, pulling out drawers and emptying them, throwing papers on the floor, opening and slamming cupboards. They grabbed Mary's phone and several items of clothing belonging to Jackson. One said that they would come back for Jackson.

They returned the baby to his mother, and they fled. The family had escaped without any injuries, but the episode left them shaking. They feared that more attacks could come—as soon as the next night.

Later, Jackson slipped back into the house. He comforted his wife and soon after called Nixon to tell him the news. He also called local police. Nixon made immediate plans to travel to Malawi. He knew the fate of his project stood in the balance. His staff was scared. Jackson told him that the night watchmen wanted to have guns and a wall built around the school. Jackson told Nixon that he, too, wanted a wall. The project's salary and benefits, which included the house, would be extremely difficult to walk away from—Jackson had found a very desirable job, by rural Malawi standards—but Jackson felt vulnerable and wondered whether he should stay.

Nixon didn't want to build a wall or bring guns. He believed it would send the wrong signal to the community and that it would make a mockery of what he was trying to do—help the neediest children in the area. But after he arrived in Malawi, he began to look at things a little differently.

His first order of business back in Malawi was to get support from traditional authorities nearby to make sure that his staff would be protected and that his project could continue. He met with Kilembe, who advised him to go to the regional traditional authority chief, who oversaw all chiefs in the area.

Again, Nixon did as he was told. Still, he was in a foul mood as he entered the local traditional authority's sitting room, which was in a village about a half an hour's drive from the NOAH grounds. In a room crowded with over-stuffed sofas and chairs, Nixon started his story with the local chief's threat and continued through the house break-in. Traditional authorities, who have jurisdiction over all local chiefs, generally resolve matters by calling in all parties and hearing their sides. At the end, the traditional authority will hand down a ruling, which must be obeyed.

The local chief appeared and told a story that was full of fabrications. Nixon, he said, had agreed to pay him, and Nixon was not fulfilling his promise of educating orphans in the area. When he finished, the traditional authority ruled in Nixon's favor, saying that Nixon had come to help the people of the area and that the local chief had, for selfish reasons, endangered this good work. He told the local chief that the violence would end. And with Nixon watching from a corner of a dark room, the traditional authority then told the chief that he would not be leading the village for much longer. In a couple of months, in fact, the change occurred. Villagers brought in a new chief, a woman who was well respected in the community. She had gotten a message from the traditional authority: Nixon's school would go on and there would be no interference. She made sure that was what happened. From the start, she made Nixon feel welcome. The old chief, Kamphambe, was furious about losing his position. But he couldn't do anything; at least not yet.

But the trouble didn't entirely disappear. In early 2007, Nixon decided to purchase five acres adjacent to the school property, giving him ten acres in all. The purchase was made after lengthy discussions with his staff. They still didn't trust the deposed chief, and they continued to push for a wall and some means of protecting themselves. Nixon changed his mind about that and decided that he would go along with their wishes and erect a brick wall. Buying the additional property would give the school room to grow as well as provide more of a buffer from the community. One of the reasons Nixon decided to go along with the wall surrounding the property was what he had observed at other schools and orphanages run by Americans around Malawi. All had taken security measures, including walls or fences. All had night watchmen, and a few had given the watchmen guns to protect the property. One director of an orphanage told Nixon that he was responsible for the safety of the children. Nixon saw logic in that, even if it made him sad to put in such security precautions.

Nixon returned to North Carolina. Once he left, rumors, some of which contained a kernel of truth, ran wild in the village about Nixon's plans to build on the additional land and erect a wall. Jackson and the others didn't know how to address the rumors and did not fully communicate the plans to members of the community. Nixon had even less of an idea about what to do, and he wasn't around to intervene directly. And so the rumors proliferated. Some people whispered that the project would soon drive all of them out. Then people talked about how Nixon's wall would block a popular walking path that went through the community; this was true, but the detour would add only a few minutes to people's walks in and out of the village. When surveyors came to mark off the land, several local people attacked one of them. Jackson called the police, who arrived and went straight for the house of the former chief, Kamphambe. Police beat up the local chief and hauled him off to jail. Nixon felt bad about the police's actions. But he also knew now that the traditional authority chief was firmly on his side. He realized that he needed to work on better relations with the new chief and members of the community.

Most of all, he needed to communicate better with them. He needed to explain the reasoning behind his plans before he set out to do them. One project that had to be explained was building the wall. Another was building a guard tower that had been requested by his security staff. This tower would stand in the middle of the property so the guards could look over the wall for approaching intruders. Nixon's feelings were even more mixed about this, but he rationalized that any organization serving children needed to make sure that the environment was secure.

Jackson hired several local men to start building the wall. Soon after the construction started, Nixon flew back to Malawi with more funds—and with a weapon, his Stevens 20-gauge shotgun. But at the airport, Malawi customs officials seized the shotgun. Nixon argued forcefully, but they said it would be released only with a government permit that allowed him to carry a weapon in the country.

In the nearly five years since Nixon had first come to Malawi, he had learned much about its culture and customs; he had also learned about the practical difficulties inherent in turning good intentions into good deeds. He was a markedly different man from the one who arrived on his first trip full of high expectations.

Although he was more humble, he was also more guarded. He looked at people warily now, especially strangers wanting to do business with him. He was just opening his school and meal program—an act intended to help the community—and yet he was building a wall and a guard tower to defend his staff and students from this very same community. He had even gone so far as to try to bring a shotgun into this community that he was trying to help.

What have I gotten myself into? he wondered. *Have I done the right thing?*

Chapter 5

Distant Struggles, Common Bonds

When Americans travel to Africa, whether to help children, start a business, or work for a nonprofit organization, it's not unusual for them to feel as though they have entered a new frontier. For first-timers especially, almost everything about traveling and working in an African country feels novel and exciting. It was no different for David Nixon, even after several trips. He felt invigorated; he was on the edge of something new and faintly dangerous. There was no script. He was forced to make quick adjustments on a daily basis and to make things up as he went along.

Over the course of a decade of traveling around Africa, I met many Americans who gushed about the feelings of excitement brought on by the risks and the slew of surprises.

I have to admit that photographer Dominic Chavez and I were drawn back to Malawi for similar reasons. Perhaps not unlike Nixon and other Americans who go on missions to help people in Africa, we felt the pull of this faraway place. Fortunately for us, we had come to know our way around from earlier trips for the *Boston Globe*, including one that helped produce a series of stories on preventable deaths called "Lives Lost." We had developed a connection to the place. So after the series ran in 2003, both of us traveled back there a few times over the years.

I also wanted to return to Malawi because the country was in the news. Madonna had begun the process of adopting a child there in the fall of 2006 and had started a charity called Raising Malawi to help support organizations serving orphans and vulnerable children. However, the finer details of her charitable work were rarely mentioned in media reports. I wasn't interested in retracing the steps of her Malawian adoption (numerous tabloids had already attempted to do that); I wanted instead to see what her charity was doing out of the public glare. Could Madonna teach us something about Western-led charity work in Africa? I had my doubts, but I was intrigued by how the organization deliberately avoided the spotlight.

And there was a third reason for our Malawi trip. A Boston-based social worker, Ellen McCurley, who had started an NGO called the Pendulum Project in Malawi several years before, was going at the same time to check on her projects. We knew Ellen well. She was a fun traveling partner and she knew many key players in the large field of aid work. Before we boarded a plane together for Malawi, she put me in touch with Penston Kilembe, who had dealt with Nixon and who also had been widely quoted as a government spokesman on the subject of Madonna's adoption.

When we arrived in Lilongwe, we sought out Kilembe immediately. He was happy to talk with us but grumpy when the subject turned to Madonna. Kilembe, a small, thin, and excitable middle-aged man whose tiny office was cluttered with stacks of files, said the Madonna adoption process was giving him fits.

"There are so many problems associated with her," Kilembe said. "And now she is thinking of adopting another child. But it's not necessary! She already has two children!"

Kilembe's cell phone rang. He spoke for a few seconds and hung up. It rang again, and he talked for another few seconds. When it rang a third time, he sheepishly turned it off. He had something he wanted to tell us, something important enough to put his phone aside for half an hour or so. He was exasperated because most people in the West saw Malawi as nothing more than a destitute place they need to save. "Everyone who comes down here has the wrong information about the country," he said. "They look at it as a devastated place, broken down. But the country is still very, very strong. The outsiders must learn how they can help before they start working."

I asked about Raising Malawi, founded by Madonna and Michael Berg, the codirector of the LA-based Kabbalah Centre, which offered courses on Jewish mysticism. Kilembe smiled and shook his head. He said the NGO was not officially registered in Malawi but that the government was aware of what it was doing. In this case, the word *government* basically meant Kilembe. "Madonna is bankrolling it, and its intent is to build the capacity of local communities in helping children," he said.

"They have good intentions," Kilembe said of Raising Malawi, "but they don't have any management structure here on the ground. They fly in and out from London. They spent two days in Blantyre, two days here in Lilongwe. That kind of organization can't be sustained if they want to do something here. Their approach is a bit haphazard it seems. I will challenge them about what needs to be done here. They have to know money cannot do everything. They have to understand that."

He said he had heard the organization was paying tribal chiefs to oversee HIV/AIDS programs. "You can't pay chiefs to deliver messages about AIDS," Kilembe said. "That is bribing them. They seem to be operating all on excitement. I even heard two, three weeks ago that they want to build an academy. We need to talk about this."

Kilembe had put Raising Malawi's executive director, Philippe van den Bossche, in touch with the Network of Organizations for Vulnerable and Orphaned Children, or NOVOC, the faith-based umbrella group. Kilembe said that I should talk with one of the leaders of NOVOC, Steve Bowler, who had been dealing with van den Bossche and others from Raising Malawi.

Bowler, who had been with NOVOC from its inception in 2002, greeted me at his home office in Lilongwe. He was exceedingly earnest and wanted to get right to business. He explained a bit about his background, and it was clear that he had a wealth of information about programs helping orphans not only in Malawi but also around southern Africa. For more than eight years, he had been in charge of an SOS Children's Village site (which bills itself as the world's largest orphan charity, working in 123 countries), and he was now working for a regional psychological support network for orphans in southern Africa as well as being chairman of the board at NOVOC in Malawi.

Madonna's charity, he said, had asked NOVOC to manage its grants. Bowler said the organization's board had many questions and concerns about the request. NOVOC was largely a coordinating body, but the Raising Malawi project would give it another task: deciding which groups should receive the grants and then determining whether the groups were meeting performance standards. Raising Malawi would have final say over all matters pertaining to fund disbursal, but NOVOC would play an integral role as a manager of the projects. Despite misgivings, the group went ahead. But Bowler said his initial meetings with van den Bossche gave him great pause.

"Raising Malawi had a classic Western approach," he said, and he didn't intend that as a compliment. He said the group had come in with its own ideas and demanded results in a short amount of time. "They wanted a two- or three-month pilot project started within weeks. Then when the groups submitted budgets, they decided to multiply the funding by four, and they wanted two-year projects."

Bowler said he and others told Raising Malawi representatives that it was moving too quickly and putting too much money into organizations, some of which operated with annual budgets of tens of thousands of dollars.

"We proposed to identify fifty community-based organizations with smaller grants, but they didn't want to do it that way," he said. "They wanted quality control on a few. What we said was true, it was the right way to go about it. We tried very hard to get them to split up the money into smaller amounts. But they wanted to demonstrate a clear impact on children. They wanted to come after two months to see impact. Well, you need two or three years to see impact."

In the end, NOVOC did as Raising Malawi asked. It picked ten community organizations, and instead of being given a $25,000 grant, each received up to $200,000 over a two-year period. The groups had varying degrees of experience. A few had budgets greater than $200,000, but others had annual budgets under $25,000. When the leaders of the groups heard they'd be getting the Raising Malawi funding, they were overjoyed and a bit dumbfounded. When they started receiving these large checks, a couple of the groups imploded due to jealousies and fights over who would control the funds. One group even disbanded, Bowler said, after it received a sum far in excess of what it was used to. The group members squabbled over what to do with the money, and the infighting grew so intense that they couldn't continue.

A second group, he said, faced a different kind of disaster. The local chief, who for months had been the unpaid security watchman for the group's orphan-feeding center, demanded to be paid now that the group had a large amount of funds. When the group refused, the chief took revenge. He stole all of the biggest cooking pots, shutting down the feeding center for three months. It had only just reopened, Bowler said, after the group relented and paid the chief wages for a job he had earlier agreed to do for free. Although Raising Malawi was well intentioned, it often sowed strife and chaos in the organizations it bestowed its gifts upon.

Raising Malawi had budgeted $1.8 million for the project over two years, and this included the $280,000 it would pay NOVOC for its role as coordinator. Bowler said the influx of money into NOVOC caused rifts in that organization as well. "Our profile was raised, and mistakes were made," he said, and he explained that much of the money went to building up the organization in order to manage the grants. The organization, he said, suddenly grew from a handful of employees to twelve staff members and became too focused on building a budget for headquarters operations instead of sticking to its original mandate of serving as a resource for member organizations. "Now we have reduced staff of NOVOC from twelve to eight, and the onus again in the organization is to push work on members and build their capacity," he said. He meant, but wouldn't say directly, that NOVOC became too concerned about building its own mini-empire. NOVOC was proud of its reputation for providing assistance to members, but people in the aid community had begun to view the organization as kingmakers of a sort. This was extremely uncomfortable for Bowler and his colleagues.

We met that night with Ellen McCurley, who told us that her organization, the Pendulum Project, had distributed about $340,000 over the past five years, almost all in grants of under $15,000, including some grants of just $1,000. We told McCurley some of Bowler's stories, and she smiled knowingly.

"I've been hearing a lot about Raising Malawi," she said. "I kind of wish Madonna had come in and talked with people first before giving out all this money. It's really important to try not to do harm, even while you are trying to do good. One question I always have is how much money is actually trying to get to the beneficiaries. I think that giving really has to be about strengthening groups that the community supports. It's not rocket science, but the way aid has been done, with a lot of money given to groups that may or may not be connected to communities, well, nothing sticks. If you don't involve the community, it doesn't get any traction."

McCurley said that, in her experience, it was best to give smaller grants to community groups. "You have to be careful with how you give out money because you can overwhelm these groups," she said. "I've seen it happen."

I left the next morning to travel around the landlocked country to check in on several organizations funded by Raising Malawi. I wanted not only to learn about the impacts of the funding—positive and negative—but also to hear from Malawians themselves about what they thought about this type of giving.

The first stop was about thirty miles outside of Lilongwe at Consol Homes Orphan Care, which had received one of the largest donations from Raising Malawi's funds. Executive director Alfred Chapomba met Dominic and me in a parking lot a few hundred yards from where he was building a center for orphans. Chapomba looked at us with suspicion, and as I started to tell him why we had requested to see him, he said, "Why should I trust you?" It was one of the hardest questions for us to answer, because trust can take time, and time was a luxury we didn't have. When I mentioned to him that Bowler had said some groups were overwhelmed by the amount of funding from Raising Malawi, he took offense.

"To say we can't absorb the money, that is more like an insult to the local organization," Chapomba said. But then he softened his stance, acknowledging that, in general, giving small groups lots of money very quickly can cause problems. "There have been bottlenecks, and we cannot completely rule out the fact that others have had problems because of capacity issues. Handling these accounts is sometimes a challenge for others," he said. That was all he wanted to say.

I understood why Chapomba was so suspicious. Raising Malawi's high profile meant scrutiny by the press, which put people like Chapomba on guard before beginning a conversation with an American writer. He wouldn't trust me until he could figure me out, and that would take a lot longer than a single conversation in a parking lot. He said we should check with the other groups, but as far as he was concerned, Raising Malawi's methods worked for his organization. He was, not surprisingly, more than happy to receive the funding to build a school and community center.

We went back on the road, heading for a group called Home of Hope. Like many countries in Africa, Malawi has more than its share of organizations with the word *hope* in their names. We even saw a sign for Hope for the Hopeless. Home of Hope was the orphanage where Madonna had found her adopted son, David Banda. His mother had died, and his father had asked the orphanage to raise his son.

The orphanage was founded by the Reverend Thomas J. Chipeta, who had lost his parents when he was fourteen years old and was raised by an older sister. His sister had taken good care of him and made sure he got a quality education. Chipeta never forgot his sister's deeds, and he felt so fortunate for all she had done for him that, after having been a pastor for forty-five years, he decided to do something about Malawi's growing orphan population. In 1992, he started inviting orphans into his home in Mchinji, which is on the Malawi-Zambia border. Five years later, the local Presbyterian church donated forty acres to Chipeta, and he went to work building an orphanage. In 1998 it opened, housing twenty children.

When I met Chipeta in the fall of 2007, Home of Hope housed nearly five hundred children and included both a primary school and a high school; it employed twenty-six teachers. He wanted to show off his campus, so Chipeta, Dominic, and I set out on a slow walk, Chipeta leaning on a carved walking stick. We passed numerous classrooms and six residential buildings. Looking inside, we saw that each dorm room was jammed with more than a dozen bunk beds. It was the middle of the day, during classes, and only a few children were visible outside, walking in pairs and carrying textbooks. When we peeked into another building, the orphanage's nursery, we heard the deafening wailing of babies. Even though several women cuddled some of them, the babies outnumbered caregivers by a long shot. Chipeta shuffled outside quickly, perhaps bothered by the din or perhaps not wanting us to see the conditions. He cared about the babies, of course, but he seemed to care more about our perception of his orphanage.

Outside, he alluded to the nursery scene, saying, "It's not so easy to keep over five hundred children, some of them small babies. We get babies one day old, when a mother dies soon after delivery."

I asked him about Madonna, but he wouldn't talk about her or about how much Raising Malawi was giving Home of Hope every year. That was part of his arrangement with the group, he said. But he did want to complain a bit about how Raising Malawi's funding had put a crimp in the group's fund-raising attempts.

"When people hear we have been helped by Raising Malawi, they think we have enough money," Chipeta said. "But we don't! It's always a problem when you're given money and that's publicized. We could do a lot more if we had more resources. I want to build our own small college."

"Then the children would never have to leave?" I asked him.

"That's right. They would stay here until early to mid-twenties," he said.

"But what about adjusting back into the greater society?"

"We are all about improving the lives of children," Chipeta said. "The more funds we have, the better we'll help them—all the way through college!"

Chipeta's enthusiasm gave me pause. But before I could engage Chipeta further, he excused himself. He had several other appointments in the afternoon and he said he was late. He thanked me for coming and then walked back toward his office.

As I walked around his campus, I wondered about the arrangements that Raising Malawi had made with its grantees. Bowler had earlier told me about problems with some of the grants, but would the grantees themselves open up? Would any acknowledge the difficulties in these slapdash arrangements? Then again, why would any group criticize its funder?

We drove from Home of Hope back to Lilongwe that night, and the next morning we walked into the headquarters of an organization called Ministry of Hope. There I met executive director Charles Gwengwe, and I immediately liked him. He seemed at ease and he welcomed my questions.

He was in charge of six community-based orphan-care centers, which provided meals, Bible study groups, medical care, and technical training. Most of the orphans, with the exception of babies in a crisis nursery, lived with their extended families. His group helped pay the school fees of 250 high school students and was looking at extending some support to those students who attended college.

But, he said, "we don't want to sow a seed of dependency. We are not for orphanages. We would rather encourage community-based orphan-care approach. That strengthens the African extended-family system. I know it's been stressed, but I think we can strengthen it. Orphanages make people feel they have given up and don't take responsibility in any way. Here, we are coming alongside you to offer you care, and then we help you within your extended family."

Gwengwe said Raising Malawi was giving the Ministry of Hope about $100,000 a year or a little less than one-sixth of his $650,000 budget in 2007. He said his experience with Raising Malawi was unlike any he had ever had before with donors.

"Everything happened so fast," he said. "There was no proper documentation for the grant. There was no MOU"—a memorandum of understanding, which is part of the typical donor-recipient agreement and spells out the arrangement and expected outcomes. "The way the funds came was that someone brought a check to this place, and we deposited it. Later, NOVOC dictated the process more and made for more formal arrangements."

Gwengwe said the arrangement with Raising Malawi made him somewhat wary of his relationship with the group. "Raising Malawi was careless," he said. "I don't see them as monitoring the programs. The whole thing was a bit of a mess."

The Ministry of Hope, he said, was going through a maturation process, and that meant exerting far more control over what kind of assistance it would take. "We are even learning to say no," he said. "If funding is not handled well, it can be an enemy to an organization. Instead of adding value, it devalues everything. When funding comes in like Raising Malawi's money, it was like a big splash. But it doesn't make one feel comfortable, and some groups who received it had no system to deal with the money. They gave this money with no documentation. They wrote a check and this was all." In his arrangements with other funders, he said, he had signed contractual agreements that detailed how the money would be used, the expected outcomes, and whether financial information related to the spending of the grant needed to be provided to the donor.

So what would Raising Malawi say to all this? Philippe van den Bossche, the director, was very reluctant to talk with me. He finally agreed to have a conversation over the phone. At the time of the call, van den Bossche said he had made seven trips in the past year to Malawi. He first wanted to talk about the great needs of orphans in Malawi.

"I spend my time in the villages with the kids, and I can tell you that the children are suffering, they are in pain," he said. "While they have smiles on their faces, they are malnourished."

Van den Bossche said Raising Malawi was guided by four main principles for helping children in Malawi: providing for direct physical needs, including food and clothing, medical care, and shelter, for tens of thousands of kids; providing support for other projects that help children, such as the Millennium Villages initiative; providing funding for programs that offer psychological and social support for children; and making sure Raising Malawi's plan fits with the country's national plan of action. "We want to support the federal government, the municipality agencies, and all the traditional authorities, including the chief or the headman of villages," he said.

Van den Bossche said that he believed Raising Malawi had proceeded with enough care, and he disputed criticism that the organization had given too much money too quickly. He said that Raising Malawi had helped not only those groups but also the entire country by drawing attention to it.

"I'm very excited that Malawi is now on the map," he told me. "Prior to our work here in these last few weeks and months, people didn't know where Malawi was. I'm happy for Malawi. What I'm unhappy about is that I wish the media would portray Malawi not as a pathetic country, but as a country brimming with hope. It's exciting to give Malawi a shot, to perhaps invite investment and support from donors. At the same time, we want to do it in a way that empowers Malawi."

Many people wondered whether Madonna and Berg would bring in their belief in kabbalah, a mystical Jewish school of thought described by the Kabbalah Centre as an "an ancient wisdom that reveals how the universe and life work. . . . It's the study of how to receive fulfillment in our lives." Van den Bossche, who identified himself as a Catholic, said that Raising Malawi hoped to introduce kabbalah as a "non-religious program meant to empower kids." The group hired eight Malawian teachers—"all Christians," he said—who traveled to the United States for three months to learn the curriculum of the program.

"They created a Malawian version of it, and then they went to Consol Homes, and went to families, guardians, and to the children, and they all agreed to take part in it," van den Bossche said. "In Malawi, people are very suspicious of any witchcraft, and the word *spirituality* even scares them. We will see if it works. If it does, we will continue it. None of it is dependent on the funding. We're offering it as a sort of service. Madonna will fund it and offer it as one of the programs."

The classes on kabbalah, he said, will "teach sharing, caring, tolerance, and human dignity. It also will identify problems and it becomes this empowerment program for kids. But we're not building any kabbalah centers and we're not planning on teaching kabbalah in any other parts of Malawi."

I left the conversation a little less than impressed. Van den Bossche seemed defensive, and he also seemed to overstate his knowledge of the situation as well as the impact of Madonna's giving to Malawi. I didn't think that putting "Malawi on the map" translated into improving services for children in the short or long term. How could Raising Malawi give the country "a shot" at success? He was speaking with great confidence about a place that he had been to seven times. Did he really know what was best for the country? And I was curious as well about the kabbalah aspect of its support for orphan care. Was it any different than what Christian missionaries had done for generations—basically imposing their beliefs on a vulnerable population? And why would he point out that the Malawian teachers were Christians? He seemed to be saying that Malawians and outsiders shouldn't worry about the influence of kabbalah in the curriculum because, after all, those giving the lessons were Christian women.

It made me think back to that first meeting that I had had with Kilembe, the Malawian official in charge of the social welfare of children in the country. Kilembe had been furious about Madonna and Raising Malawi, and he clearly saw failings in their approaches. He wasn't upset only about the circus around Madonna's adoption. He was also bothered that someone with so much money was running what he considered a poorly planned charity.

But what stayed with me from that meeting with Kilembe wasn't what he said about Madonna. To him, she was an outlier; the power of her celebrity put her in her own category. Just as U.S. government workers had previously told me to do, he said I should be investigating the scores of Americans who arrived anonymously and immediately disappeared into the fabric of society there. They were starting projects that were disconnected from the national plan to help orphans, and he wished he knew more about them, though he had recently met one helpful person he wanted me to seek out.

Kilembe stood up from behind his desk and inched past me to get to a tall stack of paper atop a file cabinet. He spent a minute, then two, then three. "You should meet this guy," he said. "Here it is. His name is David Nixon and—are you ready? Here's his phone number."

He read aloud Nixon's local cell number. "This guy," Kilembe said, "he came here and went out to a village and built an orphanage without telling us. We found out about it, and I closed it down. He accepted a plan to use it as an outreach center, a feeding program as well as a school for vulnerable children. That's what we want across the country—outreach centers that can help thousands and thousands of children for very little cost. Orphanages are so expensive and they help just a small number of children.

"Call Nixon," Kilembe said. "See what he did."

Chapter 6

A Grave Loss and
a Daunting Challenge

After meeting with Kilembe, I gave David Nixon a call. My hope was that I could persuade him to meet with me soon—even the following day. I figured we could have a brief call, maybe five minutes; I would give him the outlines of my project, and that would be that. But after I introduced myself and my work, I got something entirely different, an outpouring of emotion from a stranger. He was at a breaking point.

It was late, about nine o'clock. But Nixon didn't seem to mind my call and said there was no need to apologize, that he always worked into the night. After I told him more about my project, he sighed and said he was exhausted beyond words. His bones ached; his head hurt, he said.

He explained that he had had an especially long day, part of it spent out at the NOAH site and part of it at Lilongwe Central Hospital. In fact, he said, he had just left the hospital's pediatric ward, where he had basically camped out over the past ten days. One of the kids at his feeding center and school, ten-year-old Sautso Mathews, was being treated for complications arising from AIDS. Sautso's parents had both died of AIDS-related diseases several years before, and now an aunt was raising him.

Sautso was just one of more than 230 children attending classes at Nixon's project, but Nixon said he felt an exceptionally close bond to him. He was one of the few

children with HIV attending the school, so Nixon made a
point to ask NOAH supervisors about him whenever he was
home in the States, and he sought Sautso out every time he
visited NOAH. But the boy's illness wasn't what made him
stand out, Nixon said. It was his personality. "He is full of
joy; his face shines when he smiles," Nixon said. "He can't
run as fast as most of the kids, he isn't the sharpest in his
class, and he gets really sick from time to time, but he is still
happy." Nixon said he marveled at Sautso's capacity for joy,
especially at how Sautso was able to keep his mood up even
as his health took a major turn for the worse. It was clear the
boy was in the throes of full-blown AIDS; the hospital had
diagnosed him with bacterial meningitis and tuberculosis.
And yet Sautso was brave. He tried to keep smiling.

Listening to Nixon, I couldn't help but feel somewhat
surprised that he was divulging so much. When I introduce
myself as a reporter, most people are guarded at first. They
want to know what I'm after, and they ask veiled questions
to try to figure out my motivations. A few, though, like
Nixon, welcome the interest. Sometimes it's because the
person has been wanting to tell his story for so long that it
just comes tumbling out. But sometimes it's that the timing
is right. I call when someone needs to talk. I thought this
was what was happening now with Nixon. He obviously was
feeling deep hurt and pain, and he needed to talk about it. I
thought of these types of calls more as therapy sessions than
interviews, as I would say almost nothing and just listen
closely, gently directing the discussion while nonetheless
jotting down everything he said.

Nixon said it was as if this illness had put everything
in perspective for him once again. Saving Sautso was his
primary goal right now. "He's a poster child for what we are
trying to do here," he said. "He's the kind of kid that we

want to help out. But he's having a hard time. He weighs just twenty-nine pounds."

His voice began to falter. He took a breath. "Sorry," he said. "It's hard. But he's such a fighter, he's hanging on."

At least that was what Nixon kept telling himself. In reality, Nixon went on, Sautso had good days and bad days at the hospital, and this day had been a very bad one. His skin was so taut that the outlines of his bones were visible. The bacterial meningitis, which had taken hold in the last few days, was particularly worrisome. It is one of the most painful diseases in a country that has many dreaded illnesses, causing an inflammation of the meninges, the membrane that covers the brain. Meningitis causes these brain tissues to swell. Patients grit their teeth in pain; they moan and cry out, and in the end stages, their eyes take on a look of wild fright, rolling back in their sockets, only the whites showing. Nixon had seen Sautso endure some of this pain. It would pass, then it would consume the boy again. Every night, he would leave Sautso at the hospital and return to his guesthouse, falling asleep wondering how the boy was doing.

In Lilongwe Central, as in most hospitals in Africa, caregivers watch over patients as overworked nurses move from bed to bed. These family members and friends are responsible for feeding the sick, buying their medications, cleaning their beds, and providing comfort in any way they can. Sautso's aunt and members of her family came to the hospital off and on. Nixon was there more than anyone. But there were times, sadly, when Sautso was alone. Nixon knew he was neglecting a long list of pressing tasks that needed to be done at NOAH, but he didn't question his choice of spending as much time as possible with the boy. He became the child's advocate at the hospital, alerting nurses when there was a problem and questioning them about the treatment. But more than a week after Sautso was hospitalized, Nixon became so frustrated with the hospital that he sought outside medical help, from an American doctor affiliated with Baylor University, which had a long-established pediatric AIDS practice in Lilongwe. The doctor examined Sautso and looked closely over the boy's medical charts and questioned the nurses. He came back to Nixon with a long face. He said that the nurses hadn't been giving Sautso his medication for TB or meningitis. Nixon was furious. The doctor made sure that the boy was started on the right drugs, and Nixon couldn't help but think what this unbelievable oversight meant in terms of Sautso's survival.

"I'm ready to wring someone's neck at the hospital," he said, his voice growing deeper and heated. "I can't believe that no one gave him his medicine." I had listened to Nixon now for more than twenty minutes and was impressed by how much he cared for the boy and took everything to heart, to put it mildly. Nixon told me that he needed to get some sleep, and so we arranged to see each other the following morning. It turned out he already had plans to come to my guesthouse, which was also where two other American visitors were staying. They had planned to go out to his site in the morning, and Nixon invited Dominic and me to join them.

The next morning, Ellen McCurley, the Boston social worker, joined us for breakfast. We met the two others who had arranged to meet with Nixon. One was Karen Bruton, a former corporate executive who had formed a Tennessee-based charity called Just Hope International; much of the charity's work involved drilling boreholes to provide clean water for rural villages so women and children wouldn't have to walk miles for it. The second American was Bruton's friend Melissa DuPuy, who was shooting video during the trip to help Bruton document her work with the wells. We talked and talked as we waited for Nixon, looking at our watches as early morning turned to midmorning. We wondered what had happened to him.

They knew about the situation with Sautso and that it was weighing heavily on him. "David has really cared for this child," Bruton said. "I mean, he's been putting diapers on him, feeding him with an eyedropper."

A four-wheel-drive vehicle pulled up in the gravel driveway, and out came a man wearing a floppy safari hat, a gray shirt, and shorts. It had to be Nixon. He walked into the lobby and took off his hat, revealing his shaved head, and introduced himself.

He took a deep breath and apologized for being more than an hour late. Then he took a seat on a bench.

"I have some bad news," he said, and he paused, casting his eyes down, fingering the brim of his hat. "Sautso has died."

Then his composure broke. His lips trembled and he began to weep into his callused hands. "Sorry. I'm sorry." The guesthouse staff looked up at the scene. Bruton walked over to comfort him.

He tried to collect himself on the bench, wiping the tears from his eyes. "Because of Sautso, so many things happened to me," he said haltingly. "I'm not the typical Bible-thumper, but I'm very respectful of my Father. And Sautso was like Jesus. Everything I ever dreamed, I think, paled in comparison to saving that child's life. Everything I can think of."

He took another deep breath and started telling the story of that morning. He had received a phone call from someone at the hospital who had informed him that Sautso had passed away overnight. Nixon then called Sautso's aunt to make arrangements for a funeral. Those were now under way, he said. That done, he had to confront something less tangible: his guilt. He felt he should have done more. "It's so frustrating," he said. "If he had gotten the medicine he needed at the hospital, he would be fine now. They left him sitting on a bench. I was just holding him as he screamed for two hours. When I tried to get help for him and brought in that doctor from Baylor, the head nurse said, 'I make the decisions here, not the doctors.' I am very upset with those people. They have very strange beliefs. They seemed to prefer that he would just die."

Nixon stood up. He said he needed some air, and we had to get moving anyway if Bruton wanted to see the work on the boreholes that her charity had paid for at the NOAH site.

And so we piled into Nixon's vehicle, and he proceeded to give an account of his past five years, from the moment he arrived in a field to the local chief's threat to building the school. It occurred to me that recounting the difficulties and triumphs of his time in Malawi provided him with a temporary respite against the roiling sadness and guilt he was feeling. "When I started, I was naive," he said. "I started from scratch. I was ready to start an orphanage. I even built the orphanage, and then went to the office of Penston Kilembe, and he cut me to pieces. He said, 'No, you are not going to open an orphanage.' I remember going home that night, thinking about what they had to say, and said to myself, 'Well, it means I won't have to diaper and feed two hundred kids every night. So it's not all bad!' Still, I was very apprehensive from the start. When you start saying to people that you are going to do this, or do that, they start clinging to you, drowning you. It's been great, but it's been a constant struggle. It still is. I never know month to month how I'm going to meet payroll. Never."

McCurley, a natural talker, sat and listened, rapt. An Irish Catholic raised by her aunt in New York City, she could be tough one moment and loving the next. She was a quick judge of character and was just as curious as we were about Nixon, especially after she'd heard her friend Kilembe's read on him. Like many who have started charities in Africa on their own, she'd learned the hard way, through making mistakes and then correcting them, and she looked at others just starting out to see if they, too, had been humbled by the experience. Beneath her wariness, McCurley had great empathy for others. She knew how hard it was to get things done in Malawi, to find projects that communities supported, and to find people whom she could trust and who would work during those long months that she was away.

McCurley had told me once that going from a rich country like America to a poor one like Malawi gave Americans a false feeling of confidence. But she said that eventually that confidence faded away. One reason was that Malawi's culture was so different from our own. It's hard to understand the way people think, to figure out who has power and who doesn't, and to ascertain when faith or beliefs start to influence things. She explained that it was impossible not to be humbled after spending time here, because bad things happened, and often you could do nothing to stop them. Kids died, and you were powerless; your wealth was nothing in the face of these harsh realities.

"Doing this work in Malawi makes you realize you can't control everything, you can't save everybody. You just can't," McCurley had said then. "The hardest thing is seeing a child suffering or dying. There was a baby that I tried to save in the hospital, and the baby died. In Malawi, it's just so present, life and death, and you run around and do everything you can, but so much is out of your control. The fact that you tried, and the fact that you failed, well, you have to feel that trying is important. As long as it's trying without harming people, that's the big issue. You really have to remember to always be respectful."

I was thinking about all this as we drove past the city limits with Nixon yammering away. He seemed to need to talk—anything, I supposed, to keep his mind off Sautso. Soon the road turned to dirt. Ours was one of the only vehicles on the road, though hundreds of people walked along the route. Some boys and men carried tall stacks of charcoal either on their heads or teetering on their bicycles. Women balanced heavy plastic buckets full of water atop their heads, while children walked in fields of brush to watch over goats and cows. A sign for Nixon's project appeared on the left— the Nlira-Wanga Orphan Aid Homes—and he turned onto a road that was little more than a walking path. A few minutes later, we pulled up to the NOAH site, and Jacques Jackson, Nixon's manager, came over to greet us.

Jackson approached the vehicle with a big smile. Jackson had first met Nixon five years earlier, and since then he had assumed most of the responsibility for operating NOAH while Nixon was out of the country, which Nixon was roughly nine months of the year. Nixon saw natural leadership abilities in Jackson that he wanted to nurture. He arranged for him to take classes, including one on computers. Soon after that, Jackson was sending financial reports to Nixon on Excel spreadsheets. Nixon had started to wire money from his bank to a bank in Lilongwe every month—so he wouldn't have to carry thousands of dollars with him when he went to Malawi—and Jackson managed the money. Nixon still made most of the decisions about spending, but in a pinch, Jackson was authorized to move ahead on projects. Soon after Jackson greeted us, Nixon pulled him aside and told him about Sautso. Immediately, Jackson's features tightened.

Nixon gave us a tour of the site, showing a half-built eight-foot-high brick wall and a half-built thirty-foot-high guard tower in the middle of the site. On one edge of the property were six brick buildings and an outhouse. Five of the buildings were for classrooms, while the sixth was Jackson's home and office. A few other small homes for teachers and security guards were on the outskirts of the property. Nixon said the wall alone had cost $17,000 to build, and he had to raise money to finish it. "Most of the community supports us, but we had to do something about the lack of security here," he said. "I was advised by local police to get a shotgun two years ago. I had earlier met orphanages that were robbed by people with guns, and I found out that almost without exception anyone with a compound with children has got weapons."

The security situation wasn't the only issue on his mind. Only three weeks earlier, a group of eighteen Americans, led by his old buddy Marvin Tarlton, had come to the site with a charity called Samaritan's Feet. The group included six doctors and a dentist who were giving children checkups at every stop. They worked in a kind of assembly line, generally staying at one place for eight to ten hours. They also did a one-day blitz at Nixon's center.

The doctors and other volunteers had set up a triage center with examination rooms to do physicals on all 230 students at the school. Nixon thought this was a good idea; he wanted to make sure all his students were healthy. The group had also brought some supplies and shoes for three hundred children. But at end of the day, Nixon learned something that disturbed him greatly: the group was testing all the children for HIV. It was a complete surprise to him. He learned of it only because someone in the group gave him a box of used syringes to dispose of and told him the needles had been used for the HIV tests.

The people from Samaritan's Feet finished their work, packed up, and were gone half an hour after seeing the last child; they left before Nixon could ask for details about the tests. The group had done these tests without asking permission of anyone in the community, telling Nixon at the end of the day only that they wanted to give him the results so he could act accordingly if a child became sick. But the ethics of HIV testing are complex. By this time, I had covered many stories in Africa about the low number of people who sign up for HIV tests and had documented some novel approaches, such as volunteers going door to door and asking families if they wanted to be tested. (The door-to-door testing worked remarkably well, in fact, with acceptance rates in some neighborhoods topping 95 percent.) In these years, when treatment was just starting to expand rapidly, many Africans were reluctant to get tested at a stand-alone site because people would gossip about them and wonder whether they were infected. But I had not heard of any instances of medical professionals testing people without getting their permission first. This violated a patient's basic right to informed consent—an egregious breach of ethics. The concerns, to me, were numerous: Why didn't Samaritan's Feet ask for permission? If it was too difficult to get permission from an orphan's relatives, was it a good idea to test the child in the first place? And setting aside the violation of a patient's rights, one had to be concerned about what would be done with the information. What would they do with the knowledge that a particular child was infected? Would they tell Nixon, as they'd said they would? And what would he do with it? Would counselors be available to talk with people to help them process the test results? All of these issues should have been addressed.

Hundreds of studies and journal articles have been written about HIV counseling and testing. Countries have protocols for the accepted ways to do it; most of them involve counseling a patient before and after a test. In 2007, as antiretroviral drugs were becoming widely available throughout sub-Saharan Africa, the counseling part of the equation only grew in importance because contracting HIV was no longer a hopeless situation. There was no cure for AIDS, but the drugs could extend and better lives.

Nixon felt terrible about what had happened. He had been completely immersed in trying to save Sautso's life over the past ten days, but the unauthorized HIV tests were nagging at him all that time. McCurley listened as he finished the story and shook her head.

"I feel for you," she said. "You could be ostracized."

"It's horrible," Nixon said. "I thought they had things under control. I really need to talk with them about it. That's the danger when you have an inexperienced person with a big heart and they blast away in here and do harm."

I asked whether the group had at least some minimal counseling before or after the tests. Nixon said no. "They were running them through here, one after the other," Nixon said. "They wanted to see as many people as they could. I don't think they would have gotten permission to do the testing if they asked. They were trying to do some good, but . . . well, they didn't."

It wasn't the only issue with the group's visit, he said. They had brought three hundred pairs of shoes, but more than seven hundred children had lined up to receive them. "We had to push the crowds of kids back," Nixon said. "The police had to push them back. Eventually they decided they couldn't control the situation and they stopped giving out the shoes and packed the rest up. What a disaster."

I agreed with him completely. It was always hard for me to understand why anyone going into a different culture would give away anything—from lollipops to shoes—without working with a local partner to figure out the best way to do it.

Bruton, who was across the site, near the guard tower, called over to Nixon. We walked over to her and then to the water pump. It was just about ready for use. All it needed was a concrete base, which would be poured in over the next few days. Nixon primed the pump and soon water was coming out of it. It was a tangible benefit for the site and for surrounding families, to whom Nixon was planning to make the water available. Bruton took her turn at pumping, and water gushed out. She was thrilled, and perhaps something in that moment (or had she thought this out beforehand?) caused her to ask Nixon, "David, will you baptize me?"

"Well," Nixon said, "I'd be honored." He had a gleam in his eye. Bruton saw it, and tried to temper his vision.

"Just a renewal, David. I've already been baptized."

Nixon smiled at her. "If we're going to baptize you, we're going to the river."

I thought he was just teasing her. I thought he would baptize her on the spot. But she didn't take it that way and started to back out.

"I don't dunk, David," she said. "I'm a Methodist."

He laughed. "Well, I'm an immerser. It's all symbolic anyway, of the Lord rising."

Bruton dropped it. She wasn't going to do the river dunking. She just wanted a few prayers from Nixon as he poured water from the pump over her head. Nixon's mind was already moving on from the new water pump, but he wanted to thank Bruton. "I wash my hands of the days of no water," he said to her. "Every October, our old well would go dry, so for one or two months, there was no water, and we would have to drive to the river with fifty-gallon drums. This is a great blessing to us."

The day had already been a long one for Nixon, and it was evident that he was feeling the emotional toll of losing Sautso. He said he had to make a visit to see Sautso's aunt and other members of his extended family, and we said our good-byes and planned to meet in a couple of days for the funeral of the boy.

As Nixon left, I stayed behind with McCurley and the others. I had one bit of unfinished business as well: I wanted to meet Nixon's nemesis, Kamphambe, the former chief. Nixon had told me the story of Kamphambe and the raid on Jackson's home on the way out to NOAH. Jackson pointed out the path that led to Kamphambe's house. He himself didn't want to see Kamphambe; the relationship remained tense, he said, adding that the former chief still wielded some influence with a few people in the village. So I walked by myself down a narrow footpath surrounded by lush vegetation and trees. Just a hundred yards away from the NOAH site, I came upon his tiny mud hut. An older woman and four or five children were sitting out front in the shade. It didn't seem a fitting place for a chief, even an ex-chief. I asked for Kamphambe, and a moment later he appeared, wearing gray pants smudged with dirt and a white shirt that had just two buttons and a badly frayed collar. He pulled up a stool and I told him why I had come.

He eyed me warily but nonetheless decided to talk. "Nixon, you can't trust him," Kamphambe said. "He made so many promises to me. He kept none of them. He said he would pay for the land, build a hospital, bring electricity to the surrounding villages, and drill several boreholes in the area." He said the only thing Nixon did was drill the one borehole in recent days. Everything else, he said, was false promises.

I asked him about the attacks on the NOAH site, in particular the home invasion of Jackson's family. Kamphambe said he wasn't involved, and the matter at any rate was not a major one—just a simple expression of unhappiness with the project. Villagers wanted more from the project, including jobs, and NOAH hadn't brought anything to people there, he said.

"They are not even educating many of our children," he said. "Why can't they educate more of the kids in this village, as opposed to taking just orphans from the surrounding area?"

Kamphambe said villagers were actually quite tolerant of Nixon. He said the only incident of violence had been the result of Nixon's error in buying a plot of land adjacent to the site that Kamphambe had initially given to Nixon. He claimed Nixon had bribed landowners to purchase the second five-acre plot, and two surveyors arrived to draw the boundaries without anyone's telling the community about it. After Kamphambe and others confronted the surveyors about their work, police arrived, beat up Kamphambe, and jailed him overnight before releasing him, he said. "The reason that the American Nixon has turned on me is because I refuse to sell the original plot to him," he said. Kamphambe said if Nixon left and another American took his place, he would let him use the land, as long as he and others in the village benefited somehow.

He said he would never deal with Nixon; the American had caused him nothing but trouble. He motioned to his two grandsons who had dashed out of his house. "They must walk three miles to their school when there is a school right in our backyard," Kamphambe said. "I want them to go to that school, but [Nixon and Jackson] refused."

Now, the ex-chief said, the situation was about to become much worse. He nodded his head toward the property. "See that wall?" he said. "That wall is going to cause lots of problems."

He wouldn't say anything more. It felt like a threat.

I decided to seek out other families nearby, including those whose children were attending the school. More than 230 children were enrolled at the school at the moment, and Nixon planned to add another grade the following year, pushing the enrollment up to more than 320. When I walked back from the ex-chief's house and entered the NOAH site, I visited a couple of the classrooms. The children had smiles on their faces, and unlike many primary school classrooms that I had been in, the teachers were not leading the students in class-wide exercises of learning by rote and repeating answers after the teachers. Instead, especially in grades four and five, the teachers called on individual students, who each stood, answered the question, and sat back down. In those older grades, teachers had between ten and twenty-five students per class, a very low number for schools in rural Malawi. I went to the fifth-grade classroom, which had just eleven students, and my eyes kept turning to one in particular, ten-year-old Robert Phiri. He raised his hand at every question and he always had the correct answers. When the class ended, I asked him if I could return to his home with him. I wanted to meet his extended family and talk with him out of the school setting. He seemed to have the ability and willingness to speak a little bit about the school; most children his age were too shy to talk with a white foreigner, but Robert quickly agreed and led the way. He was one of only two students from his village, Kadolo, who were going to the school.

"There are a lot of jealousies from people who cannot send their children to the school," Robert told me as we made our way to Kadolo, a thirty-minute walk. "But we try not to pay attention. We know we are lucky."

Robert's parents both died before he reached his first birthday. In the subsequent years, no one had told him the causes of their deaths or even much about the characters of his mother and father. We arrived at his home, a collection of thatched-roof huts, in which he lived with his great-uncle Robert Bestala Kadzakao, seventy-eight, and several other extended-family members. The village of Kadolo wasn't much, just fifteen families at the end of rutted path. It was a classic rural Malawi community: it had five bicycles total, ten cows, six sheep, six goats, twelve chickens. No one owned a tractor, motorcycle, or car. "We are too poor for that," Kadzakao said, laughing at the question of whether anyone drove a vehicle. The village had never sent one of its sons or daughters to a university.

Robert's great-uncle said that the boy's parents had both made it through eighth grade. Robert, listening to the conversation, spoke up. "I cannot tell what my future will be, Uncle," he said, "but my desire will be to complete secondary school, then university." The great-uncle looked away. Standing nearby was Robert's fourteen-year-old sister, who had married a twenty-year-old man a year before. The elder man looked at the young teenage girl and noted his disappointment.

"They are both too young, but what can you do? I advised her not to get married, but she threatened to run away and get married anyway."

He turned back to Robert, who was waiting patiently for him to comment on his statement. "We don't know what will happen to you, but I am glad you want to do better, so you can go to secondary school, or even beyond, and help your family," he said.

The boy smiled and slipped away to a knot of friends. The old man turned his attention to Nixon's influence on the area. Many didn't like him and said bad things about him, Robert's great-uncle said, but he believed in Nixon. He said those who doubted him were upset because he didn't meet their expectations of a white man. They expected a white visitor to be so wealthy that he would give out food and money. But Kadzakao said that wasn't the right way to think. He said that people had gotten addicted to handouts and needed to look at outside charities differently. He said they should simply be happy that someone like Nixon cared enough to come all this way to help some of them. The longer that Nixon stayed, Kadzakao said, the more that people would understand that. He had no doubts about him. He also had no concerns about Nixon's rules stipulating which children were eligible to attend his school. Nixon had to draw the line somewhere, at least for now, he said. He believed that Nixon would continue to help more people.

"The American has a heart like Jesus," he said. "He stays to help us. You can see that very clearly. Just look at the school, and just look at this boy here."

We were soon on our way back to Lilongwe in a four-wheel-drive vehicle that McCurley had arranged for. McCurley was deep in thought about the day's events. Nixon, she noted, was dealing with a lot of pressing problems. She was particularly troubled by the group of Americans who had come in and done HIV tests. Sitting across from me in the back seat, McCurley looked out the window at the scrub bushes and shook her head. She turned to me and said that so much went on during days like the one in which the six American doctors came in and checked out the children's health that Nixon couldn't have known everything that was happening. Also, he seemed to have his heart in the right place, and that counted for a lot.

"He's got an element of craziness in him," she said, flashing her crooked smile. "I like that. You've got to be a little bit crazy. It's the only way to keep going. You know the people doing a lot of these projects, jamming along, are faith-based people. They will put themselves on the cross for their work, and die for it. They also don't question stuff, and just go on their faith. I guess it's easier that way—you don't have these huge internal struggles about whether you were actually doing good or not."

She said that the big questions facing Americans in Africa were rooted in the work of the missionaries who had started coming more than three centuries ago: What was the purpose of coming to Africa? Was it ultimately to convert Africans to Christianity? Or was it to follow the example of Jesus Christ and help relieve others' suffering? Or was it something else entirely? Was it for more self-interested reasons? Was it more about the person who went, rather than about the people in Africa? McCurley was raised Catholic and didn't identify so easily with evangelical Christians like Nixon, whose motivations were so openly linked to their faith. She had a more detached and less grandiose view about why she had come to Malawi. She believed she had come because she was trying to help people, and everywhere she turned she could see people who needed help. But sometimes she wondered about her motivation—sometimes it wasn't so clear.

"You know, so many people ask me and others, 'Are you trying to save souls in Africa?'" McCurley said, sitting in the back seat of the vehicle, jostled by the ruts in the road. "And I always tell them, no, that's not what we're about. We may be only trying to save our own souls."

▲ ▲ ▲ ▲

Two days later, I met Nixon at Lilongwe's central hospital, which had recently been renamed Kamuzu Central Hospital, for Dr. Hastings Kamuzu Banda. In 1964, Malawi achieved independence from Great Britain, and Kamuzu Banda became the country's prime minister. Kamuzu, a U.S.-educated doctor believed to have been born at the end of the nineteenth century, was the principal leader of Malawi's nationalist movement and governed Malawi from 1961 (when it was known as Nyasaland) to 1994. In 1966, he was elected president of Malawi and later declared himself president for life, establishing an autocratic regime that kept the country a one-party police state. Despite his heavy-handed rule, he was viewed by many Malawians as the country's founding father, and naming institutions, such as the hospital, after him was a way of honoring the nation's history since independence.

Nixon planned to meet us in the back of the hospital, at the morgue. From a trip we took here in 2002, Dominic and I knew the morgue all too well; we also knew the mortician, Daniel Chikuse, a portly man whose eyes I could still picture with haunting clarity. They were yellow and clouded, jaundiced. He was in charge of the records book that listed the names and details of bodies that were checked into the morgue and then checked out by relatives, and I remembered Chikuse sitting outside in the sun one day, writing down the release time of a body (the woman's name was

Rebecca Makwenda, she was twenty-six, she had AIDS, and she had died fifty minutes after entering the hospital). As he wrote, he said, "Death, death, death; every day, death."

Just walking up to the morgue brought back memories of so many people we'd met during those two weeks in 2002. McCurley, in fact, had joined us for part of our time in the hospital, and there was a very ill sixteen-year-old boy named Nenani who had fallen in love with her; he said he dreamed of going to America and kept asking if she would take him. He was a talker, a charmer, and we all fell for him. He had a tumor growing behind his right eye, and he died a few months later. Then there was a couple, Wilson and Cecilia Casis, whom we met at the hospital. Cecilia had full-blown AIDS, and her five-month-old baby, Angelina, weighed five pounds. Cecilia couldn't breast-feed because of her weakened state, and the parents couldn't afford baby formula. I remembered McCurley arranging for a friend to take the baby and try to nurse her back to health with baby formula. The father, Wilson, was so grateful; Cecilia was so weak that she couldn't talk, but she understood what was happening, and she looked McCurley straight in the eye and seemed to convey that she appreciated all her efforts. And I remembered the child dying two days later, at 4:30 A.M. on a Sunday. The caregiver had stayed up all that night trying to save Angelina and then wept the entire next day.

I tried to look at the morgue from two perspectives. One was through the eyes of those who worked there, and for them, it was all about systems, routines, and following all the proper procedures. For them, this was not an emotional place; this was an orderly place, and their job was to keep it that way. But for visitors coming here, their time in the morgue ranked among the most emotional moments of their lives. It was a place to wail. Not weep—wail. Women would take over the back end of the morgue, a loading dock–like area in which broken-down trucks, station wagons, even donkey-pulled carts—anything that had a flat bed to carry a body—would pull in. And after a few short words by some of the mourners, or maybe just a great deal of wailing, the vehicle or cart would pull out, and the trail of mourners would follow.

Before that, though, women and men would arrive and position themselves in the back of the morgue. Next, a small entourage of three to six people would enter the morgue, produce documentation that showed they were related to the deceased, sign out the body, and then, wearing latex gloves, wash the body on a stainless steel bed. Watery blood would fall to the floor. After the washing and drying, the relatives would dress the person in the finest clothes they had, which they had brought with them, and then carry the body out to the makeshift hearse. When they appeared outside carrying the body, the wailing would always rise to meet them. Sometimes women would faint or scream out to God or to the deceased, and waves of pain flickered across everyone's face. It was unbearable to watch. The piercing cacophony of suffering often brought tears to my eyes. Or sometimes I just walked away.

I was prepared on this morning at the hospital morgue. I knew what to expect. I was sure Nixon didn't. He had possibly been to a few morgues in his life but he hadn't been to Kamuzu Central's, and he surely had never come to a morgue to pick up the body of a boy who seemed like Jesus to him.

Nixon arrived with eight members of Sautso's family. Four family members entered the one-story morgue, which kept bodies in three walk-in freezers. I followed behind and asked for the mortician, Chikuse, but an attendant told me that it was his day off. I watched them pull a tiny body off the shelf in one of the freezers, and then I went outside to find Nixon.

He was still fuming about the death. Coming to the hospital had brought back all his anger. "This place just makes me want to scream," he said quietly but forcefully. "The nurses were absolutely militant about what you could do and couldn't do and they just let the child lay there and ignored him."

Inside, meanwhile, the relatives washed Sautso's body, dressed him in black pants and a white shirt, and placed him inside a wooden casket, which Nixon had bought that morning from a roadside coffin maker for twenty-three dollars. They closed it and brought him outside, and Nixon walked up to greet them. Some of the relatives began to cry and moan, and Nixon calmly asked if he could open the casket to say a prayer. There was the body of tiny Sautso. The one detail that stood out above all else for me was, oddly, that his eyelashes were extraordinarily long.

Nixon bowed his head in prayer, and the others lowered their heads with him. "God," he said, pausing and putting his right hand on the chest of the boy's body, "don't let this death be in vain. Do something with this child's life. I trust you, Lord, I trust you."

Nixon started to weep, and his face became wet with tears. Still, he kept his wits about him. He wasn't as overwhelmed as I'd thought he would be. Sautso's family also looked to him to make the logistical decisions around the funeral. Maybe it was because he had taken such interest in the boy, or maybe it was because he was seen as more powerful than they were, but they didn't seem to mind that he was quietly getting things moving at the morgue and preparing for the long slow drive to the village for burial.

Later, after they all arrived at Sautso's aunt's house, Nixon asked for a moment with the body, and he placed some things next to the boy's body that he believed Sautso would have loved: a coloring book, pencils, a small toy car, and clothes.

In the aunt's village, more than 150 people gathered to walk the last quarter of a mile to the graveyard. A truck carrying the coffin led the procession down a steep hill and then up another hill, and then the mourners turned left off the road to walk into the cemetery. Some people wept. Some sang hymns. Everyone seemed to know where to go in the graveyard, to the side farthest from the road, where three gravediggers, shirtless and streaked with sweat, waited with their shovels. They had dug a hole five feet deep. A group of men brought the casket to the grave and slowly lowered it into the ground.

After about thirty minutes of singing and prayers, people walked up to the grave and each threw a handful of dirt atop the casket. Nixon joined them. Then the crowd dispersed. Nixon was ready to go as well. He had only a few days left in Malawi before returning home, and he had several things to do; he felt, more than ever, that people were depending on him.

In many ways, they were. On the day of the funeral, the local chief at Sautso's village, Banti Masula, sixty-two, told Nixon that he had made a great impact on the area. The village had about a hundred orphans, and thirty-six were enrolled in the NOAH program. "It is helping a lot with nutrition and education of our children," Masula told him. "A lot of families want their children to go there. We have been talking to you about sending other kids, but not just orphans, to the school, but so far we've had no luck. We will keep trying."

Nixon told the chief that he very much understood the need for better schooling but that he had limited space and funds and did not want to overwhelm his teachers and hurt the learning process. He said he would do the best he could.

The next day, I traveled with Nixon out to the NOAH site. He had called a meeting of his workers to talk about any unsettled issues. He said he held such meetings two or three times during every trip. The meetings served many purposes: they gave workers an opportunity to bring up issues that troubled them, and they gave him a chance to understand the dynamics of the project a little more.

At the start of the meeting, held in one of the classrooms, he told the fifteen staff members that the biggest issue remained security. He said he felt the place was more secure now that the tribal authority had arranged for the local chief to be replaced; the new chief was supportive of them. "The tribal authority brought in all the local village headmen, and they talked for four hours one night with just a candle illuminating the room," Nixon had told me earlier. "They argued and fought, but in the end they all agreed we had done everything right. That we had signed papers for the land, we had taken those papers to the land bureau in the city, we had registered it." Now, he said, he was in the process of finishing the purchase of a second five-acre tract of land that would allow the project to expand. Some of the family members had moved off the property, but some were refusing to go. He was preparing himself for another long land dispute.

He told the staff that the project was about to get large shipments of food from USAID; NOAH would be distributing this to ten communities over the next year. Nixon had bid on the project to generate a little income to keep the school operating and because it fit within the mission of his project. But Nixon needed to make sure the food was secure and wouldn't be stolen. He told the group he wished he had the brick wall and the guard tower finished, and he wished he had his shotgun. But he was putting the matter in God's hands. "I don't ever forget that it's God who has protected this place," he said. "Our safety does not come from walls and guns. It comes from God. The Scripture says that a horse is prepared for battle but safety comes from the Lord."

Jeffrey Mademba, a watchman, raised his hand. "It's very important for us to have a gun," he told Nixon. "If there is a rumor that there's a gun in the community, they will be afraid to come here."

A second guard, Bokola, who had led the funeral for Sautso, responded. "If you hadn't been a strong believer in Jesus Christ," he said to Nixon, "you would have stopped this project. God already has shown his power in keeping us open."

Nixon thanked him, but then turned serious. He said he himself had an important issue to raise. He wanted to make sure that confidential information about the school and feeding programs remained a secret within NOAH. He feared that outsiders would use that information to carry out disinformation campaigns in the community. "One thing I want to say to everyone is about our policy of confidentiality and unity on staff. Any employee sharing confidential information outside the community at the very least will be suspended. All of us know that there are a few people in the community looking for an opportunity to take advantage of us. So no information discussed by the staff should be discussed in the outside community. We love the people here, we work hard to help the people, and no one can say we think we are more special than anyone else," he said. Later that

day, Nixon made a courtesy visit to the traditional authority head, Masumba Nkhunda. Nixon had developed a close
bond with Nkhunda. The first time the two had met, Nixon
had related a parable from the Bible. "It was about the mustard seed planted in a farmer's garden and how it grows until
it becomes a tree," Nixon remembered. "The mustard seed
usually produces a plant. But the farmer allowed it to have
uncontrolled growth on the body of Christ, allowing birds
to come in and build nests." Some biblical scholars have interpreted the parable as a metaphor for the growth of Christianity, but Nixon perceived it differently. He told Nkhunda
that he saw the parable as a warning that if a farmer does not
perform his duties, he will lose control of his garden.

In the same way, he told Nkhunda, "If you teach against
polygamy and the use of alcohol, you can't as a chief go get
drunk in the middle of the night or take many wives." As
I got to know him better, I learned that this kind of comment was pure Nixon. He was unafraid of insulting anyone,
perhaps to the point of being undiplomatic. What was important to him was to relate the word of God as he understood it. In this case, he had made just the right point. After
the mustard-seed story, Nkhunda asked everyone except
Nixon and Jackson to leave. He told the two men, "God
has brought you here today. I am an evangelist myself, I
have one wife, and I don't drink." That night, the three men
talked about God, leadership, and the principles of govern-
ing. They had made an important connection.

For this visit, Nkhunda appeared in the small waiting
room and hugged Nixon. He thanked him for all his work.
Nixon thanked him for his support and told him about
Sautso, about the new wells, and his plans to expand the
school by one grade in the coming year, which would allow
him to enroll a hundred new students.

Nkhunda was pleased. But he encouraged Nixon to do more. He had a formal way about him, which was reflected in the way he spoke. "If the people in America want to help us, let them help David Nixon in his efforts to help orphans," Nkhunda said. "So many people are looking for your help, David Nixon; we are just waiting to see. We are expecting more, more, and more, but maybe not knowing what all of us will get."

Nixon laughed at the thought of doing more, more, and more. He was barely able to keep up the pace as it was. He thanked Nkhunda and promised to see him on his next trip. He was on the last two days of a thirty-four-day trip, and he had so much more to do. He had added up the expenses, and it seemed daunting to him: $1,300 for shoes and uniforms for a hundred new schoolchildren (uniforms cost $8, shoes $5); $7,000 to install two more wells; $7,000 to construct a warehouse and a classroom building; $12,000 for a new truck; $1,850 for the final payment of a solar-powered energy system; $1,500 to complete the guard tower; $17,000 to finish the brick wall; $300 for two-way radios and flashlights for the guards; $2,500 to improve the homes for five new staff members; and $300 to survey the land. Excluding the security wall, he figured he needed to come up with $33,750 soon. He had some funds lined up, but was still $10,250 short.

He went to bed that night thinking about how he would raise the funds. He couldn't think about Sautso right then; he needed to focus on the project. Nixon prided himself on his ability to solve problems. When he faced a problem, he saw himself as unstoppable, able to stay up day and night until he found a solution. And when he had a problem involving children, instead of getting angry and violent, as he had as a young man, he thought about how Jesus would act. He realized that he was harboring a great deal of anger about the death of Sautso, about the way the nurses had botched his care, and he knew that he had to keep that anger in check. *When Jesus was cursed, he didn't lash out,* Nixon thought. *When Jesus was physically punished, he didn't retaliate. Instead, he responded with love.* For the past decade, Nixon had been asking God for guidance, for help in turning his anger into forgiveness. He needed to know how he could bear the death of Sautso.

Chapter 7

The Lure of Orphanages

After hearing David Nixon's backstory about his initial plans to build an orphanage and how he'd been forced to abandon those plans, I wanted to delve deeper into the question of whether orphanages were appropriate options for Americans wanting to help children in Africa. It was no secret that orphanages had a horrible record in the United States and Europe, where long ago institutionalizing children had been abandoned in favor of placing them in foster homes and then permanent homes. But that didn't deter many American faith-based groups. There was something about seeing children wearing tattered, dirty clothing and not going to school that made these groups want to scoop them up and put them in a clean home with running water and working toilets and send them to a school with only thirty or forty other "rescued" children in a classroom.

In late 2006, prior to meeting Nixon, I had attended the Global Conference on AIDS at the Saddleback Church's Lake Forest campus in Southern California. At this gathering of two thousand representatives of mainstream American evangelical Christian churches that wanted to help children in Africa, I met people from all over the United States; some had large ongoing projects in Africa—many of them orphanages—and some were seeking advice on how to start projects.

Walking onto the Saddleback campus felt a little like entering an alternate universe, especially after I had spent the past three years living in Africa. Palm trees provided pools of shade around Saddleback's spotless 120-acre campus, which was so large that it had an information desk to direct the conference-goers. A giant cross rose above a worship center, which could seat 3,500 people and, like many megachurches, had large TV screens flanking the stage so those far away could see what was going on. In back was a team of technicians working the audio and lights. In a megachurch, as on Broadway, the stage production was critical.

The attendees were cheerful and positive. They seemed energized by the possibility that they could make a huge difference in the lives of some of the most vulnerable people in the world, AIDS orphans. The AIDS conference was led by host pastor Rick Warren and his wife, Kay, and it had drawn two U.S. senators, both of whom would soon be running for president, one of them successfully: Sam Brownback and Barack Obama. They came not only because both political leaders had placed AIDS and Africa on their list of global priorities but also because of the substantial political influence of evangelical Christians on the 2008 race. And then there was the specific influence of Rick Warren, the author of *The Purpose Driven Life*, which gives readers a forty-day spiritual journey to follow and which had sold nearly 30 million copies at the time of the conference. One survey had asked Christian leaders which books had been the most influential in their lives, and *The Purpose Driven Life* was the most frequently named.

At the conference, both Rick and Kay Warren talked about the importance of doing something to fight the AIDS epidemic, but it was a couple of other talks that really got my attention. One plenary speaker spoke of a tiny church in Texas that had adopted thirty-six children from Africa in the previous two years. He exhorted the crowd to spread the word of the church's mission to adopt and to encourage others to do the same. Later, at a side session on orphans in Africa, which attracted an overflow crowd, a speaker talked about the joy of starting an orphanage, which he said ensured that children who were malnourished and wearing raggedy clothes suddenly had three meals a day, running water, beds, an education, and a loving home. The second speaker, a pastor, told stories about how "heroic" members of tiny churches in Texas and Oklahoma began adopting children by the dozen. He said they were saving the lives of the children, doing God's work.

I looked around the room and saw a lot of people nodding in agreement. When the speakers asked for questions, I wondered if anyone would challenge them. Finally, toward the end, one did. A woman with long red hair raised her hand. She introduced herself as Kerry Olson, the founder of Firelight Foundation, which was started in 1999 with more than $10 million that her husband, Dave, had earned during the dot-com boom. Her philosophy was to support communities and listen to their best ideas to attack the orphan crisis. Olson started to gently question the speakers' messages. She said that she found the best way to help kids in Africa was to listen to what communities wanted. And most communities, she said, wanted to keep the children in the communities—not put them in orphanages or send them overseas for adoption.

She could understand how outsiders seeing such poverty would want to do something—anything—to help out. But she said that when people went to Africa, they should look closely at scenes unfolding in front of them, and in particular look at the interactions among families. "No one ever sees the relationship between the child and the loving grandmother," Olson told the group. "But that love means the world to the child, and that should be preserved whenever possible."

After the meeting ended, I caught up with Olson. It was a beautiful sunny afternoon in Southern California and as we talked about the session, she said she wondered if anyone was really listening to her. From her stack of papers, she pulled out a Firelight Foundation booklet called "From Faith to Action" that described how some of the faith-based groups her organization funded in Africa were involved in providing services to families and children. She said she was flabbergasted by what she had heard at the meeting and surprised at the lack of push-back from the audience.

"I just don't understand how they could say that churches should build more orphanages," she said. "It's really disturbing to hear speakers at this conference tell people that, because you know that will influence many churches' decisions on what to do. It's a constant battle to get this message out to help local community groups because they really do know what is best for their community. They live there!"

Over the next two days, I talked to many people at the conference. They were excited about doing something in Africa, and they talked about countries where they wanted to go, contacts they had, and orphanages they knew about. They just wanted to help children.

When I started traveling around Africa the following year, I spent time with many Americans working on projects. They included, in addition to Nixon, a couple from California who helped street kids in the western Kenyan city of Kisumu addicted to sniffing glue; a couple from Oklahoma who adopted a baby in Rwanda; and a young man from Virginia who had grown up in poverty, later earned advanced education degrees, and then raised funds to pay the school fees for fifty children in Ethiopia. They were representative of thousands of people like them and I was amazed at their devotion and commitment to helping the less fortunate. Traveling with them, I felt I was in the constant presence of heroes whose work was not celebrated or even recognized and who might never be known outside the circles of their friends and acquaintances, save perhaps by a handful of people in the volunteer community. But being celebrated wasn't the point for them. They were doing this because of a spiritual conviction that they must help these vulnerable children.

Each had a story about what motivated him or her. The couple from Oklahoma, Dave and Melissa Osborn, who adopted a nine-month-old boy they named Ethan, put it well: "Sometimes, as Americans, we are coming and thinking we can solve the problem, or maybe help solve part of it," Melissa Osborn said. "We want to help in any way that we can, and right now we're doing that for Ethan by giving him a home."

I also met many people in the faith-based movement who built or worked in orphanages. One of the most ambitious orphanage projects was a Ugandan organization called Watoto, which means "children" in Swahili. Uganda was experiencing a significant increase in the number of orphanages opening. One survey showed twenty-two orphanages in the Mukono District in south-central Uganda alone; the entire district's population was just 450,000.

Watoto, though, was much greater in scale than any one of those. The group was established by Canadian Pentecostal missionaries and funded mostly by Americans and

Canadians. One U.S. official working on orphan issues described Watoto as a kind of "Disneyland in Africa," an orphanage so separate from the daily lives of most Ugandans that it had the feel of a walled-off land stripped of the reality around them.

In Watoto's headquarters in Kampala, co-founder Marilyn Skinner, who with her husband, Gary, had come to Uganda in 1993 to start a Pentecostal church, was gracious and warm in welcoming me. She got right to the point about their choice in starting Watoto.

"God spoke to my husband, Gary, to look after children," she said in her spacious office. "Gary didn't want to look after children. But then we read Psalm 18, extolling the Lord. We started a small single-family dwelling for orphans after that."

Skinner said that "the words leaped off the page" from Psalm 18, which reads in part:

> *In my distress I called to the Lord;*
> *I cried to my God for help.*
> *From his temple he heard my voice;*
> *My cry came before him, into his ears.*
> *The earth trembled and quaked,*
> *And the foundations of the mountains shook;*
> *They trembled because he was angry.*

She said they interpreted the passage as a message from orphans crying out for help. They felt the government of Uganda could not do this work alone, and it needed outsiders like themselves to do something.

"The problem with Africa is leadership," said Skinner, who was not bashful about expressing her opinion. "There's really a leadership crisis here. So in caring for orphans and widows, we really wanted to make leaders out of them. The AIDS crisis made this situation too big for the government. It was too big for the World Health Organization, too big for the World Bank, too big for the NGOs. But it's not too big for the church. The church is a force."

The Skinners started planning an orphanage, which they grandly and optimistically called a village. As it turned out, this proved to be an apt description, for by the end of 2008, Watoto was home to 1,633 children. Watoto's annual report said it raised the equivalent of $11 million in 2008, with $6.5 million in operating expenses. That meant it cost roughly $4,000 per child per year, making it a Cadillac of orphanages in sub-Saharan Africa. Its finely honed operation was impressive. In 2008, it raised money from 12,264 individual sponsors. It sent five choirs to Australia, Asia, the United Kingdom, the United States, Canada, New Zealand, and Europe, each for five- or six-month tours, complete with school tutors. One choir sang for the Canadian Parliament. Others recorded an album with the Grammy Award–winning Christian musician Chris Tomlin.

Its centerpiece property—the so-called Disneyland—is called Suubi Village. It sits atop a hill about twenty-five miles from Kampala. When I drove up the road toward the site, the view suddenly opened to reveal a 360-degree view of the valleys below. I felt like I had arrived at an elite U.S. prep school. Spread out over the hilltop were administration buildings, classrooms, and athletic fields. A choir was singing in beautiful harmony in one of the rooms, and a few dozen children were playing a spirited game of soccer on a playing field.

School officials gave me a quick tour of the place, starting with the housing for the orphans. Eight children live in each house with a "mother"—often a widow who has been hired to oversee the orphans' lives. After the tour, I sat down with several students. Classes were over for the day, and the children were sitting in the sun, enjoying the downtime.

"We don't feel like we're in an orphanage," said a girl named Blessings. "They give us new brothers and new sisters. Somehow it feels like a boarding school."

Sitting next to her was a girl named Stella, who said, "It feels like home. I get everything I need. I eat every day and I'm healthy."

"I feel the same," said Angela, fourteen, whose parents had died and who was the youngest of their seven children. "I needed help before I came here when I was nine years old. My family moved me from house to house, from aunties to uncles. But here, I feel I am at home. I like to hang out with my new brothers and sisters. And since I don't have a real mother, the mother in my house is like a mother."

The girls had traveled the world as members of one of the choirs. Angela had been to Washington, New York City, Baltimore, Quebec, and Scotland, where she had performed before parliament members.

"We are the blessed ones," said Stella. "Many people outside of Watoto never even get to school."

When I left the school, I drove down the hill and stopped at a village called Nakirbe near the valley floor. Right by the side of the road was a collection of small structures. This was the village's public school for children in the first six grades, called the Golden Age Community School, which amounted to a small grouping of tiny open-air buildings with dirt floors and worn wooden benches. Chickens ran about the place. Dogs slept in the shade. The village, a collection of mud huts, was all around it. There were no playing fields or playgrounds or much of anything outside the classrooms except for a small eating place for teachers. Mukasa James, thirty, walked over and introduced himself as the headmaster. A huge crowd of young children gathered around us, and he apologized for the commotion. He said he had 156 students attending his tiny, open-air classrooms. School fees per student were the equivalent of $27 a year. The total annual school budget for all the children was about $4,000—or roughly what it cost for one Watoto student to go to school for a year.

"We want to be like them. We are forever trying to contact them," said James. "When you go up to their property, it's like going to the United States. I've never seen such a school like that one. The classrooms are all beautiful. The children have good seats. They have toilets. It's very modernized."

Watoto had donated a few supplies to the Golden Age school, including five wooden blackboards, geometry sets, rulers, red pens, and a wall map of Uganda. "We appreciate it," he said. "And we don't want any money from them. But it would be nice to get materials. We would like to build a whole new school—enclosed, with walls and a roof—here, and the people of the village would build it themselves."

James said he had many orphans at his school. He didn't know the number, but he said it was "dozens." Rain started to fall, and he and the children ran into one of the classrooms. The roof leaked and water fell onto one of the wooden benches in the room.

Roosters crowed in the background. James looked at the sky and then at all the children around him. "We do our best," the headmaster said with a shrug.

The stop at the village school provided a stark contrast to Watoto. It made me wonder why Watoto had chosen to take care of relatively few children as opposed to helping many more with its abundant resources. Another issue was whether the experience ultimately was the best even for the children who stayed at Watoto. There was no doubt they would receive a better education, but would their experience prepare them for life after the orphanage?

The U.S. government clearly didn't think so. In the early days of the PEPFAR program, some U.S. funding did directly or indirectly support some orphanages, but that was phased out after a couple of years. Instead, PEPFAR funneled increasing millions of dollars into other types of orphan-care programs. Congress earmarked 10 percent of all funding to support orphans and vulnerable children. In fiscal year 2008, that translated to $399 million in PEPFAR's fifteen focus countries, twelve of which were in Africa. It was a major escalation of funding. Three years earlier, when PEPFAR was just getting off the ground, it spent $83 million for orphan care. The funding had increased nearly fivefold in three years.

It was almost certain that the sum of money spent by U.S. churches for orphans amounted to more than PEPFAR's and USAID's budgets for child health (which combined were under $1 billion a year). What concerned U.S. officials was that the private and public efforts were working at cross-purposes.

Dr. Beverly Nyberg, senior technical adviser for orphans and vulnerable children in the Office of the U.S. Global AIDS Coordinator, said that the U.S. government wanted to discourage the building of orphanages. She said faith-based groups' promotion of them was a major concern.

"It is encouraging to see that so many groups want to do something," she told me in an interview in Washington.

"There is a lot of interest in supporting orphans in particular. One of the difficulties has been that often the faith-based approach has been to build orphanages. Research has shown that orphanages are not the best way to care for children; they are not the best approach to foster child development. This is particularly important in the younger years. Children in orphanages have generally less stimulation, which affects brain development. While they may get fed better and get better schooling, what they really need is to be loved, touched, and interacted with. While there is a lot of love out there, there may not be enough to go around in an orphanage."

Nyberg said she hoped that faith-based groups could harness their energy and direct it toward supporting community centers, schools, and other efforts "that help build the community, as opposed to taking kids out of the community. In many of the orphanages, there are children who are put there by their parents thinking they are doing something good for their child. They want to give them more schooling, better nutrition and clothing—more than they can give their child in those areas. But bottom line, an orphanage does not give them a family."

She said she once asked a group of community volunteers who oversaw a range of orphans services in Mozambique what they thought their greatest contribution had been. "One woman replied, 'You can't tell the orphans from the regular kids anymore.' That was great. That really is our end goal. We want all kids cared for in families to get the same love, care, and support their own kids get. That is one of the principles we try to get across."

Nyberg did see specific niches in which orphanages could positively contribute, including places of rescue for newborns and places of transition for street children. But she said that often when a young child entered an orphanage he or she didn't leave until age eighteen. "They should be more of a holding tank while those who run orphanages work to get the child in a family," she said. "That's what we're trying to emphasize right now, that the orphanages can be a means of facilitating moving these kids into homes as quickly as possible."

That's what had happened years before in a large group of orphanages in Ethiopia. The Jerusalem Children and Community Development Organization started in 1984 with the mission of opening orphanages around the country. It eventually ran six orphanages that took care of roughly a thousand children in all. But in 1996, the association reversed course and decided to close down the orphanages and reunify children with their extended family in communities.

In Addis Ababa, Ethiopia's capital, I sought out Bayable Balew, a program officer at the organization. Balew said the association began to doubt its mission after monitoring the children who reentered communities.

"We don't encourage anybody to build an orphanage because we learned about the many disadvantages," he said, sitting in his office at the organization's headquarters in Addis. "Orphanages are not a sustainable solution, first of all. We also found they create psychosocial disorders for children. They create dependency—not only for the children, but also for the community. Members of the community started bringing children to orphanages instead of dealing with the children themselves."

He said the orphanages became islands of relative privilege; children there generally had better living conditions than did children in the community. But, I asked, wasn't that an argument often used by supporters of orphanages—that they provided advantages such as education and nutritious food?

Balew nodded. "Yes, generally, you could say they get medical care, food, TV, schooling. Children don't want to lose it. If you give them a choice, most will want to stay in an orphanage as opposed to staying in rural areas. But [in] our experience in reuniting the children with their families, we found something that children lack very much in an orphanage: family love. They get none of that love when they are away from their families."

He said that when eighteen- or nineteen-year-olds left the orphanage after completing secondary school, they almost always had significant adjustment issues. They didn't fit into society, he said. "They had major communications problems. They didn't know how to interact in social situations. They didn't know what was expected of them in the community," Balew said.

In addition, people in communities didn't know how to deal with the children who had just left the orphanages. "There is stigma and discrimination against them," he said. "The community kind of isolates the children. It is difficult to mix the children back into society."

Over more than a decade of reunifications, the association had placed all but twelve of the one thousand children back into their extended families. It spent a great deal of time reunifying the children with their families and reintegrating them into communities, and Balew acknowledged that it was a long, difficult process. He said the best way for me to understand would be to talk about the process with a child who had gone through it.

He made a phone call, and the next morning I met Berhanu Aba, twenty-six, a handsome young man who had spent a decade in one of the association's orphanages. He had been on his own for six years. Over tea, he told me his story. He and two sisters were put into the orphanage by an uncle after their parents died.

Berhanu said he felt comfortable in the orphanage but didn't realize how comfortable he was until he left it, at age twenty. He shuddered at the memory of leaving it. He said he felt like a stranger in his own land.

"Even our traditional coffee ceremony, I didn't know anything about it," he said. "I didn't know how to greet people over coffee, or how to interact with them. I felt afraid of everyone. I lost my confidence. I thought that people would criticize me, so I didn't have the courage to speak up. I always felt like I was doing something wrong. For three years, I was very confused and alone."

Berhanu acknowledged that for the most part he felt like he had managed to build a life for himself after leaving the orphanage. His two sisters were in Addis Ababa, and for a time he lived with them and supported all three of them. The orphanage had helped train him in printing skills, and he was working for a printer, earning about a hundred dollars a month, a livable wage in Ethiopia.

Even though he said he was happy, he still felt the effects from his decade in an orphanage. He continued to feel out of sync with others. For instance, he said many of his friends had girlfriends, but he did not. "I would love to have a girlfriend," he said. "But I'm too shy to say anything to a girl. I prefer to stay quiet. I don't know how to be around them."

Berhanu had to leave, and he politely excused himself. For me, he represented something that Americans coming to Africa rarely saw: the hidden cost of orphanages, revealed by a person who had lived in both worlds and who had had so much trouble outside the orphanage's walls. While many

Americans strongly believed that orphanages would save children and build the next generation of leaders, Berhanu and the many others who reentered Ethiopian society after years in orphanages represented a group of young people who clearly struggled in the real world. Their years of cloistered living may have given them a better education and training in trades, but it failed to give them the tools they needed to live on their own and according to the customs of their country.

Chapter 8

A Matter of Faith

All Americans who go to Africa to help children, whether
they build orphanages or adopt a child or start a school,
have one thing in common: they run into unforeseen difficulties. So it was with David Nixon. After five years on the
Malawi project, his life was about to get much more complicated and challenging. He would have to grapple with
the realization that his understanding of the foreign culture
around him, and his judgment of its people, was a lot less
astute than he had given himself credit for. Because of mis-
placed trust, he would have to make choices that pained him
greatly. Like Job, Nixon was tried time and again, and he
too wondered whether God was testing his faith. These trials exposed his weaknesses, and he needed to learn whether
he could turn those weaknesses into strengths.

The problems weren't just in Malawi. They were also
waiting for him back home in North Carolina, as he discov-
ered soon after we parted ways following Sautso's funeral.

In Monroe, Nixon was at a loss. He had just returned
home from a thirty-four-day, emotionally taxing trip in Malawi—perhaps his most difficult trip in the five years of his
work for children there. The death of Sautso haunted him.
Nixon blamed himself, even though everyone told him it
wasn't his fault and that he had done as much as possibly
could have. His friends assured him that his example of trying to save a boy's life had had a big impact on those around

him. For the teachers and staff at his school in the village in Malawi, and for villagers at the funeral who watched him closely, it reinforced how much this American cared about the children and about his project. Many, out of respect, had given him the nickname Father Noah.

On the surface, the project was in better shape than ever before. By the middle of 2008, it had grown to about 350 students in the school, twenty-three local workers on staff, and a budget of more than $9,000 a month. It had become a large operation, and the bigger it became the more it made apparent Nixon's most glaring weakness: he couldn't consistently secure the funding needed to support its rapid growth. Nearly each month, Nixon felt like he was scrambling. The year before, in 2007, he had tried something new. He bid on and won a $375,000 USAID food distribution contract. While almost all of it went to pay for the food and for shipping it to the NOAH site (that alone cost $310,000), Nixon had some left to pay salaries and expenses and to cover the cost of building a small structure to hold the food. The project, though, quickly turned problematic. The shipments were originally to arrive in the fall of 2007, but the dates kept getting pushed back, all the way to the spring of 2008, which meant that he had to distribute the same amount of food in half the time.

▲▲▲▲

In North Carolina, Nixon had to make a quick transition from Malawi back into work. He and a couple of partners had started a fledgling software company that was selling an item for schools that had, among other things, a sensor that could take children's temperatures. But the project was still in the pilot stages, and cash was slow in coming. Nixon funneled any extra income he generated back into his Malawi project.

He wasn't without support, both spiritual and emotional. One major comfort to him was that he had joined a small congregation of Messianic Jews in Charlotte. Its pastor served as an inspiration to him. Another major source of support came from his mother, Elizabeth Bridges, who was enjoying an intellectual rebirth in her later years. She invited her son to speak at a child psychology class she was teaching at a small Christian university in North Carolina. Nixon was happy to do it. He showed a videotape of his mission, which included footage of Sautso's funeral. It proved too much for him. He stood off to one side of the classroom and put his hand over his eyes and wept. Some students, overcome by the story and by the sight of Nixon grieving, also started to cry. Later, several would write in their class journals that the presentation was one of the most moving they had experienced.

Bridges watched her son closely that day and the following weeks, realizing that his experience in Malawi, especially with the death of Sautso, had changed him for good. But she knew that there were things weighing on him. In fact, the largest issue in his life had nothing to do with Malawi.

Instead, it was about another child—Nixon's own flesh and blood, his grandson Ethan, who was just three years old.

For the previous two years, Nixon had been dealing with episodic crises swirling around the boy. He didn't even know he had a grandson until one of his sons returned from military duty in Iraq in 2005 and told him that he had fathered a child who was now eight months old and living with his mother, a former girlfriend. His son also had a second child, a girl, with another ex-girlfriend.

When he received the news of his grandson's existence, Nixon immediately sought out the mother and arranged to see Ethan regularly. Ethan's mother was barely getting by, and so Nixon also started paying many of her bills, including rent, electricity, and car repairs.

Gradually, Nixon's son began to show some interest in getting to know Ethan. He asked his ex-girlfriend if Ethan could stay with him for a weekend; she reluctantly agreed. It turned out horribly, and Nixon realized that he would have to take a more active role with his grandson. At the time, Nixon was traveling to Africa at least every six months, which meant that twice a year or more he would disappear from Ethan's life for four or five weeks at a time. More and more, he felt uncomfortable with that. One night late in 2007, he received a phone call from Ethan's mother saying that a man in the Pennsylvania trailer home she was living in had backhanded Ethan in the mouth. Nixon told her to leave immediately. She did so and found a place to live outside Charlotte, North Carolina, near Nixon. But soon there were more issues. Nixon heard she had a serious drug problem. Concerned that she was capable of doing great harm to the child, possibly out of neglect, Nixon contacted a lawyer. The lawyer said Nixon had no legal standing. She had full rights.

Nixon hung up and prayed—for his grandson's safety and for the mother's good sense. He prayed she would seek help for herself and bring Ethan to him.

She called an hour later.

"I want to tell you the truth," she told Nixon. "On one hand, I hate you, but on the other, you are the only person I can trust." They agreed to meet, and when they did, she agreed to sign over her parental rights to Nixon. That would enable him to petition a court to be the legal guardian of the boy. Nixon now had a roommate, his three-year-old grandson. He had little idea of how to raise a three-year-old, at least not in the day-to-day sense. Before, he usually had Ethan over to his house one or two nights at a time, and they felt comfortable together. But having a young child over for a night was a far cry from having him over for good. Nixon had just accepted a responsibility as great as any in his life, and that included supporting 350 children in faraway Malawi.

Taking in Ethan, he knew, would have implications for his project in Malawi. He wasn't sure how he could do both. Nixon had the good sense to grow worried about the great pull of divided loyalties and responsibilities, but good sense didn't provide any easy answers. Yet he had no doubts that he had made the right decision. He had to protect his grandson. Through documents prepared by his lawyer, Nixon became the child's temporary legal guardian and would act as gatekeeper to decide when Ethan's parents would be allowed to see him.

"It's just like what is happening with me in Africa," he told me over the phone one night soon after a judge granted him temporary custody, with Ethan safe asleep in Nixon's rented house off a blacktop country road. "In Africa and here in my home, you have to defend the child. If I didn't do that, who would do it?"

Still, it didn't mean all was well with him. He very much needed to return to Malawi. After long talks with his son, Nixon decided to place the boy with him and his wife while he was in Africa. Nixon was wary, but he decided he should trust his son. He needed to put faith in him.

Nixon turned his attention back to Malawi, back to fundraising, and back to overseeing the USAID food-distribution program. "My life has consumed me," he told me on the eve of his trip in February of 2008. "I've purchased my ticket to

Malawi, I've arranged for my lodging, but other than that, I don't have any money in reserve. I am going to Malawi now on my faith. It's a matter of faith. You would think that I would be raising money as much as I possibly could for the last two months, but I haven't been able to do that at all. My main priority has been giving my grandson a safe new home."

Things had gotten so hectic that Nixon forgot to pay his health insurance, and his policy was canceled. He decided to set aside the $1,500 he needed for the policy and use it to periodically reimburse his son for expenses related to Ethan, hoping that would lead to better care for his grandson. But not having health insurance worried him greatly. In the past year, he had suffered abdominal pain so intense during preparations for a trip to Malawi that he stopped packing and fell to his knees. A doctor gave him antibiotics, and he was able to pull through it. Since that scare, Nixon had stuck to a vegetarian diet and stopped drinking coffee; this seemed to be working.

The trip to Malawi in early 2008 went well. Among other tasks, he spent a lot of time with Jacques Jackson and his deputy, Victor Chinkanda, talking to them about leadership and management of the operation. When he returned to the NOAH site in the Chakwindima village, he often heard about issues not from Jackson but from other staff members. Jackson rarely delivered bad news, in part, Nixon believed, because he wanted to show Nixon he was in control of the situation. This, Nixon told him, was not how to be an effective manager. To be a good manager of the Malawi project, Jackson had to be open with him, whether the news was good or bad. Despite that shortcoming, Nixon felt, Jackson was in a good position to lead the organization.

"Over these last few years, I've gotten to know Jackson's strengths and weaknesses," he told me when he returned. "I see his potential, and I also see he is human like the rest of us, and he has his failings. But I've become very close to him and his family. We've tested each other's patience, but that's the reality of life. We have had many heart-to-heart talks about our relationship, and in the last year, I've been talking to them about the real need for another American, someone I would hire, to go there and be a liaison between Jackson and the government of Malawi and correspond with American donors through photos and reports. Jackson has been resistant to that. I've gently tried to get him to agree." I wasn't sure why Nixon needed an American on the site, except perhaps to have someone who could better communicate with him and act on his requests in a more timely and efficient manner. I could understand his frustrations, even though he would be best served in the long run with Malawians running the entire project. Then it could last. But Nixon was in a particular bind because he wasn't there often enough, and he clearly had some misgivings about allowing Jackson to continue to run the program himself. It could have been a competency issue, or it could have been something else.

Nixon recounted one troubling moment with Jackson. He couldn't get it out of his mind. The two of them were walking in a large marketplace in Lilongwe while their vehicle was being repaired. Suddenly they saw dozens of people racing in their direction, chasing a man. They caught him, threw him to the ground, and ripped off his clothes.

Nixon asked Jackson what was going on. Jackson said the man must be a thief.

"They are going to kill him—we have to do something," Nixon said.

"No, stay here," Jackson said. "Stay here."

Some threw bricks at the man. Others hit him with sticks. Twice, there was a lull in the violence and it appeared the mob would let the man go, but then someone would hit the man again and that incited more rounds of beatings. Some people gathered straw and sticks. Nixon thought they were about to burn the man alive.

"They are going to kill him," he said to Jackson again, much more urgently.

"No, they are not," Jackson replied. "They just want to teach him a lesson."

"Someone has to stop this," Nixon said, inching closer to Jackson's face, his own face getting hot.

"If you get involved, you will be next," Jackson said.

"Are you saying you're letting fear get the best of you, and you're going to let this man die?" Nixon shouted.

Jackson looked away. Nixon looked at the man, who was bleeding. Nixon didn't know what to do. Could he, as a white man, stop the mob if he approached them? Or, as Jackson suggested, would the mob turn on him? He used his phone to call another American living in Lilongwe, who, after being apprised of the situation, also told him to stay clear of the mob because there was no predicting what could happen and that Nixon's skin color offered no protection in such circumstances.

"Pray with me then for this man's safety," David said over the phone.

They prayed and Nixon looked around him—ten or twenty people had gathered around him. They sensed he was agitated. He asked those near him if anyone had the number for the police. Someone gave it to him. He called and called—busy each time.

"This isn't right, this isn't right!" Nixon said, fuming. He looked at Jackson in frenzied disbelief. It was like Jackson would accept seeing someone die in front of him. He kept thinking Jesus wouldn't allow this to happen. He told

Jackson he was going to drive to the police station. He got in the vehicle, rushed there, and found police officers who agreed to go to the scene. But by the time they arrived, the crowd had broken up, and the man who had been badly beaten was gone. Jackson, too, was nowhere to be seen.

Nixon and Jackson did not talk about the incident for the rest of Nixon's trip, but for Nixon the episode wasn't forgotten. He just didn't know what to say. He had to process it. He thought to himself that his trying to save the man was perhaps the reason God had sent him. He may have been the only person in the whole marketplace who had that reaction. He thought he had to challenge this way of thinking in Malawi, and push home true Christian values in the name of Jesus.

But from my experience in Africa, I think that Nixon's instinct to intervene, while admirable, would have put him in grave danger if he'd followed through. Jackson was right. If Nixon had gotten in the middle of the gang, they could easily have turned on him, and then there would be no escape. On a few occasions in my travels around Africa, I have seen mob attacks, and I've slipped out of the way as quickly as possible. Once in northern Uganda, I witnessed several people beaten to death by stones and bricks after a protest had gotten out of control. At that moment, I was watching from inside a locked compound, and I knew that if I tried to intervene, the odds were good the mob would simply turn on me.

Despite the tension with Jackson, Nixon largely felt comfortable about leaving him and, to a lesser extent, Victor in charge of the project. Both seemed to value his input and took direction from him. "I believe they trust me immensely," Nixon told me. "That is not the case of other American missionaries. I don't think it's because I'm better than anyone else. I think it's because I'm more real to them—I can get upset, I can be demanding, but I will do anything in the world for them."

He laughed. "When some people are just flawed enough, just honest enough, you trust them," he said. "They are just real."

Nixon was feeling good about the state of his project. He believed it was running well with local people directing it on the ground. I wasn't so sure. I wanted to see the project when Nixon wasn't there, and I wanted to hear what Jackson and others thought of Nixon. I had the feeling that Jackson in particular was chafing about parts of the arrangement. Nixon had a strong personality and had high expectations. And his literalness about the Bible spilled over to a somewhat black-and-white view of the world. The episode of the mob beating was one example. It was wrong, clearly, and Nixon's view was that Jesus would have intervened and therefore he and Jackson should have done so. Because they hadn't intervened, they had failed to act like Jesus. Nixon couldn't shake that thought; Jackson had moved on, I'm sure. For Jackson, it was part of the inner compass he used to survive in his country.

I made arrangements to visit later that year, and I arrived at the NOAH site on a Sunday morning in late spring, just in time for the three-hour service at the Endless Life Church, a concrete structure with a tin roof. This was the building put up by Jackson and members of the congregation when Nixon first visited, back in 2002. People packed the church. Every inch of wooden bench was taken. Jackson, wearing a suit, and his wife, Mary, stood in front of the congregation as the choir led them in a rousing set of songs for Jesus.

"Hallelujah!" Jackson shouted out after the songs were over in a voice that had far more force that I'd imagined he could muster. "Give a big hand for Jesus!" The congregation clapped enthusiastically. In one-on-one meetings, Jackson was quiet and respectful. He almost never raised his voice. But here he was shouting loud enough to be heard out in the bush. His message was about what people should expect from God.

"We Christians should not expect material things," he said to the congregation. "And that means no blessings of food, or clothing, or money. The blessing from God is to be redeemed. When we are talking about blessings, we think of the cars or clothes or all kinds of things we can get material benefit from. But God is talking about eternal life, and Jesus is your personal savior."

"Amen, amen, amen," people shouted back.

Afterward, Jackson gave me a tour around the project. Quite a bit had happened since I was last there. The school had expanded to include another seventy to eighty students. The USAID food had arrived and many NOAH staff members were working to distribute it. And Jackson seemed fully in charge in Nixon's absence. I told him of my many conversations with Nixon about Sautso and about the plans to keep adding more children to the project each year.

Jackson said that the death of the boy had created quite a stir in the surrounding villages. It wasn't so much because of the death but because of Nixon's role in the funeral. "With the culture here, when an orphan dies, the surrogate parents are responsible for everything," Jackson said. "The community was very happy with what Brother Nixon did after Sautso died. Malawian people think that whites are not as responsible as they are. But he showed that he is not like all white men. When we were there, with the casket, he kept asking me, 'Is it proper to open the casket?' I asked the chief if it was proper, and the chief said, 'Yes, it is proper. The child is yours.'"

I wasn't surprised to hear Jackson asking the chief for permission. The chief is generally the most respected person in a village, and it would be imperative to ask the chief for permission to do anything at a public event like a funeral. But it was surprising to hear Jackson report that the chief considered the child to be Nixon's. I wondered if this was just an expression, not something to be taken literally. Or had Nixon made an inroad so deep that an African chief considered him the father of an African boy? Was he Father Noah to the chief as well? I asked Jackson what the chief meant.

"Let me tell you why he said that," Jackson said. "In reality, the people were not that concerned with Sautso. His parents passed away. He was sent to another relative. When we were opening the school, I talked to the grandmother of the boy to see if Sautso would attend, and she asked if we would pay for things for him. We provided clothes for the boy, and I told her all she had to do is give him a place to sleep. Brother David showed he cared for the boy—really cared. He was his caretaker at the hospital. People saw that. He cared more than anyone else cared."

Jackson said, though, the whole funeral experience had had a few unpleasant twists. Nixon had alluded only to some tense moments with Sautso's extended family, but Jackson gave details.

"We put in the coffin clothes we bought for Sautso, beautiful clothes, a jersey, trousers, a toy car, and a kind of a doll," Jackson said. "David had bought them in a shop in Lilongwe. But in the house, they took the new clothes off

Sautso and they put old clothes on him. The car, the doll, all of that was gone as well. David and I talked about it and I told him about the grandma—whenever I would give something to Sautso, she always took it. When I told him that, he said, 'Is that your culture?' I said, 'No, it is not.' I told him the grandmother didn't want the new clothes to go with the one who died but to stay with the living."

"Okay," Nixon told Jackson. "But we bought it solely for Sautso."

Jackson said he told Nixon: "We can't do anything. We're at a funeral. The grandmother is respected in the village; we cannot do anything. It is not your fault."

Nixon turned silent, Jackson said. He seemed to be growing more wary of Malawians, and actions like the grandmother's wounded him. But he was well aware of the effects of poverty in the lives of everyone in the rural communities. It was sacrilegious to him to remove the new clothes and the toys, but it could have been an act of desperation, he believed, or maybe the gifts were just so foreign to the culture of villagers.

"I know his heart was not happy," Jackson said, looking back on the funeral. "But he couldn't do otherwise."

We talked a bit then about his relationship with Nixon. He said he appreciated all that Nixon had taught him but that each of them had played the role of the teacher. Sometimes Nixon taught him things; sometimes he taught Nixon. Sometimes they were like brothers. Others times, though, he said, Nixon clearly was the boss.

He, too, remembered vividly that day in the marketplace in which the mob began to beat the thief; he remembered the tension that grew between them at that moment.

"His point was to save the person," Jackson said. "It was a good point. But I was looking after my life. In that situation, instead of gaining or saving a life, you can lose your life. Maybe Brother David hasn't gone through such situations. Maybe he also feels he will not allow someone to die in his presence. But had he entered that mob, I can tell you what would happen because I have seen it happen before. The mob will stop concentrating on the thief. It will start considering that new person and focus on him. They will start throwing stones at him. Maybe twenty, thirty, forty stones coming at once."

Although Jackson didn't get upset easily, he certainly was upset now. Reliving the episode made him remember just how close Nixon—and perhaps Jackson himself—had been to approaching the mob and putting themselves in danger.

"After that situation, we didn't sit down and talk about the event," Jackson said. "I knew that maybe I could embarrass my brother."

His voice had an edge.

"I can teach him things," he said, before adding quickly, "and I feel I have a lot to learn from him too. But to him, there are so many things for him to understand from our culture, or in connection with our culture."

I didn't doubt him on this point. Nixon could only know so much. He was an outsider, and his knowledge had been gained from his experiences in Malawi; five years into his project, Nixon still had much to learn, as I'm sure Nixon himself would have acknowledged. But Jackson was implying that Nixon didn't know as much as he thought he did—a different thing entirely. In a way, I really felt for Nixon. He wasn't living in Malawi. He was in the country perhaps two or three months a year; the rest of the time he was talking with his managers a couple of times a week over the phone. He had to place so much trust in Jackson especially, and yet he couldn't just go along with everything that Jackson said.

He had to be able to make his own judgments. He wasn't an uninformed American anymore, though. He knew his way around, but he didn't know as much as Jackson. And Jackson, it seemed to me, didn't appreciate a boss who sometimes didn't follow his suggestions.

The next day, I returned to the NOAH site, and Jackson introduced me to Sautso's older brother, Mapeta. In Chichewa, *mapeta* means "last finishing," or the last expected child. Mapeta was fourteen, three years old than Sautso, who was last. *Sautso*, in Chichewa, means "problem," implying problems with the delivery.

Jackson said that Sautso wasn't a very good student because he was often sick. Mapeta, on the other hand, was one of the top performers in the fifth grade.

Mapeta was much taller than his brother, slender, with a big smile. He, too, had those long eyelashes that I had noticed on Sautso. He said that after his father died five years before and his mother died shortly after that, he and his brother moved in with relatives. He was still staying with them, in the same bedroom he had shared with Sautso and three others. He said he thought about Sautso every day. "I read the Bible to help," he said. "It is written in the Bible that we will all die. So I try to think about that when I think about Sautso."

He said at the time of Sautso's illness, during his last two weeks of life, he couldn't believe that Nixon was with his brother every day. "It was amazing to me to see a white man be very close to an African boy like my brother," Mapeta said. "He really had a strong love for my brother. Now I feel all white men are just good people. Even I would like to take that example of what he showed me, on how to treat others."

In the hospital, Sautso would tell his brother that Nixon had bought him a new blanket or had gotten him food from a falafel place in the middle of the town. "He was very happy about it," Mapeta said. "Someone was giving him some comfort."

He learned of Sautso's death on the morning of the funeral. He accompanied his extended family to the hospital morgue, and he was next to Nixon when Nixon opened the top part of the casket lid that revealed Sautso's head and shoulders.

"I was so sorry, I just cried," Mapeta said. "At first, I was sorry that I saw him. I was extremely upset. I walked away crying. That night, I was just afraid. It was my first time to see a dead body. In our culture, children are not allowed ever to see a dead body. I was so frightened. I was thinking to myself, *Will I die like that?* In the room where I slept with Sautso, I kept seeing his body."

I said good-bye to the boy and to Jackson and headed back to Lilongwe, an hour's drive. I left feeling that Nixon had made a huge impact on a number of people's lives, especially on the children who were educated at his school. But I also sensed that not all was well in Nixon's relationship with his staff, particularly with Jackson. Perhaps it was Nixon's long absences and the inherent difficulties in trying to manage a project long-distance via Skype, e-mail, and Western Union. But perhaps there was more to it. There seemed to be some deeper tension between Nixon and Jackson that went beyond their disagreement in the heat of a mob taking vengeance on a thief. I didn't have enough information, but my sense was that Jackson had revealed that he wasn't completely happy with the relationship. It was true that both men had a fondness and respect for each other. But the relationship wasn't quite right. For both, frustrations toward the other were close to the surface.

I had no idea how close.

Two months after my visit, Nixon received an e-mail from Victor that accused Jackson of a long list of misdeeds. The e-mail alleged that Jackson regularly loaned money to staff and then charged 25 percent interest each month; that he had started work on construction projects around Lilongwe and was using the organization's vehicle for long periods on those projects; that he kept a night watchman on the payroll for two months after the watchman had left the job; and that he had closed down the school for a month without telling Nixon.

Nixon didn't know what to do at first. The accusations were so specific that they had the ring of truth to them. But Victor could have other motivations. Did he want to unseat Jackson so that he, Victor, could run NOAH from Malawi? Nixon wasn't so sure. He decided that he had to make an unannounced visit back to the project and he had to do it soon. He couldn't tell anyone. He wanted it to be a surprise inspection, and he could use the USAID food contract as a ruse, saying he needed to check that the deliveries were being made as promised.

After arriving in Lilongwe, he decided that he would interview people alone, with a transcriber and translator.

One by one his staff members entered a room that he had cleared for the purpose of the interviews. He questioned night watchmen, cooks, and Victor; the teachers would be next. He saved Jackson for after the teachers; he wanted Jackson last. The interviews lasted an hour or two, sometimes longer. At the end of one week, Nixon had interviewed many of the twenty-three staff members. Several said that Jackson had told them not to talk about any problems at NOAH and that if Nixon asked about issues, they should lie and say everything was fine.

Jackson approached Nixon at the end of the week and asked how it was going. Earlier, Nixon had decided he wouldn't confront Jackson until he had as much information as possible. But he felt an overwhelming urge at that moment to—in his words—"take him out to the woodshed, and that's what I did. I grabbed him by the arm and took him around the house."

"This is getting bad," Nixon said to Jackson. "A lot of people are pointing fingers at you."

Jackson immediately pleaded with Nixon not to do anything drastic, to keep the church and the school alive for the children.

"I want to ask you one question," Nixon said. "Did you gather the staff after I arrived and have a meeting and tell them to lie to me?"

Jackson paused. "Yes, there was a meeting, but I didn't tell them to lie—I said not to stir up trouble," he said. He said Dennis Chagunda, another person on the staff, also suggested that no one should cause trouble. He began to cry and beg for mercy. He asked if he and Nixon could go somewhere to talk privately, away from the project.

"Considering our relationship, I am going to let you talk to me privately, but you better tell me the whole story," he told Jackson. "I'm already skeptical, already upset, and you are already in trouble. You have one chance to open your heart and tell me the truth."

The next day, Jackson drove to Lilongwe to the apartment where Nixon was staying. He appeared humbled as he entered the room.

Nixon started right in with questions.

He asked Jackson if he was using the NOAH vehicle for personal projects. Jackson said only once, when he had hauled three loads of bricks to one of his properties because he had been told he would lose the land if he didn't start to build on it. Jackson denied keeping the night watchman on the payroll for two months after he was fired and charging 25 percent interest on loans he gave to staff members.

The two men talked for a couple of hours and Nixon left the conversation thinking that Jackson was guilty of little more than poor judgment. But Nixon wasn't finished with the interviews and continued holding them the following week.

The next Monday, Nixon called in Jackson and Jackson's closest ally on staff, Chagunda, an older man who served as NOAH's clerk and bookkeeper.

Nixon asked Chagunda all the same questions—about the watchman, the personal use of the car, the interest rates charged to staff—and Chagunda denied everything. Nixon turned to Jackson.

"Well, Jackson, you told me that at a staff meeting Dennis told them they should lie to me."

Chagunda looked terrified. Nixon could see he was in agony. He could almost sense the thoughts going through Chagunda's mind. Should he trust Jackson? Was his job in jeopardy?

Next, Nixon took out the attendance register and the accounting book and found the watchman's last day was May 2. But the accounting showed he was paid for May and June.

"Why did you pay him for May and June?" Nixon asked.

Jackson paused, and then confessed. He said he kept the watchman on the payroll to pay back loans from the watchman. He admitted charging 25 percent interest, and under questioning from Nixon, admitted that he took the payments at times from the staff's paychecks. "It's not a problem," he said.

But Nixon had heard from several staff members that it had become a huge issue; some of them owed Jackson more than their monthly salary because of compounding interest. Nixon told Jackson it was common sense not to loan money to people under his supervision.

"You also don't lend them at twenty-five percent interest," he told Jackson. "The Scripture says it's an abomination to God if you are not helping them out of bondage but are leading them into bondage."

Jackson said he knew of no such section of Scripture.

"You are either incompetent or a very bad liar," Nixon said.

Nixon asked Jackson where he'd gotten the money to loan in the first place. Jackson said that other churches and Americans were assisting him financially. But Nixon doubted him. He couldn't find any records that documented the loans. He was beginning to suspect that Jackson was using the money that Nixon had wired to the project as the source of the loans.

Nixon next interviewed the teachers. Several talked about the loans with high interest. And some leveled a more explosive charge: one of the teachers had been dating a twelve-year-old student, and Jackson had covered it up.

So Nixon brought Jackson and Chagunda back into the room.

"You guys are still lying to me," Nixon told them. "I need the truth. I'm really sick of this whole thing. I need the truth, Jackson, or you are done at NOAH."

This time, Jackson became defiant and turned uncooperative.

Nixon asked him if he'd tried to cover up for the teacher who dated a student.

"If that's what you think," he said.

Nixon asked if he had taken money that he sent for NOAH projects and used that to make loans.

"If that's what you think."

Nixon asked Jackson to leave. Chagunda, now alone, started telling his version of the story to Nixon. He said Jackson had instructed him specifically to lie about the watchman. Now Nixon looked at Jackson differently, not as a brother anymore but as someone who was more interested in making money than in being a Christian. He saw a side of Jackson that looked slick and shady and ready to blame anyone else.

The next day, he gathered two friends—one an expat and the other a prominent Malawian—in Lilongwe. They had been involved in Nixon's investigative project for the month, listening to him at night recount what was happening. They agreed with his recommendations. He would fire Jackson, Chagunda, and the teacher involved with the student.

That night, Nixon wrote a long e-mail to me about what had transpired. He focused first on Jackson.

> *I love him and his family with all my heart but he is not fit to lead and I suspect now that I really don't know him like I thought I did. All of the testimony is recorded and if I didn't have it to read, I would think it was all a very bad dream.*

He was particularly exasperated that Jackson would plead ignorance to some of the most serious charges:

> *How can you be ignorant about an illegal relationship with a student and a teacher and rather than defending the child, you throw her to the wolves and give the teacher more responsibility and unrestricted access to other girls? How can you be ignorant that your people are suffering and that you are hanging*

more stones around their neck with your illegal interest, not to mention that the Scripture is clear that this is forbidden among Christians? How can you think it is OK to issue payroll for someone who is gone and put the money in your pocket? I don't think he is that incompetent, he is too bright and logical. I can only conclude that he is fully aware and knew what he was doing all along. He may have rationalized it somehow but he knew. I hope he will connect with some full time missionaries here who are interested in helping him and getting him back on track.

After receiving a letter from Nixon notifying him that he was fired from NOAH, Jackson sent out an e-mail to many of NOAH's supporters saying that Nixon treated him unfairly and without forgiveness. *My family suffered so many years fighting for the peace of the children at NOAH,* Jackson wrote. *Chiefs, armed robbery, thieves have attacked my family severely, but we resisted in order to make NOAH exist.*

As for the girl who had a relationship with a teacher and then was sent back to her village, he wrote,

After I discover the relationship, I asked the girl, [and] initially she was denying the relationship but later on she agreed. I explained the issue to her guardian at my home land Ntcheu. The guardian told me to bring back the girl coz if she get pregnant I will be answerable.

Jackson disputed the story that the girl was married to a much older man. *She is married, not old man as some people may say. There is evidence that she is married because of poverty.*

His objections included Nixon's giving him no warning or written notice that he could lose his job. He said that he wanted back some personal possessions, such as

220,000 bricks that he and his wife, Mary, molded, as well as stacks of firewood.

These are my sweat not his sweat, Jackson wrote, the last, and most eloquent, line in the letter.

In the next few days, Nixon began assembling a new team of leaders, led by Duncan Phiri and Zack Nkhata. Both had worked in NGOs, and Phiri was a specialist in issues dealing with orphans. Nixon, meanwhile, needed to go home. His son and his wife were not doing well. They would go through stretches of providing a supportive home for Ethan, and then things would spiral out of control again, fueled by drugs and alcohol. Over the next few months, Nixon allowed his son to see Ethan a couple of times a week, in the afternoons, as long as Nixon was present. And that seemed to be working out fine—at least for the time being.

In early 2009, Nixon sent out an e-mail to his friends and supporters of the Malawi project. It was a difficult note to write because he had to explain what had transpired with Jackson. He didn't shy away from telling the story. In fact, he was brutally honest about the difficult moment it had been for him.

Although very little money had been misused thanks to tight financial controls, the whole accountability process, requiring two trips to Africa one month apart and involving many unplanned expenses, wiped out our reserves.

By then the financial crisis that was hitting the U.S. had also affected the Malawian economy.

Over the six months from August 2008 to January 2009, our donations were down by more than half and our expenses in Malawi had inflated to more than double. In a

*few short months we have gone from being sound, to being
in peril. Having said that, we are still able to feed, educate
and provide medical care for an orphaned child for about
$25 a month. We just need much more support to be able
to do it. Multiplied by 360 children, that comes to $9000
a month, not including long term expenses such as vehicles,
maintenance and minimal development for sustainability.
Our main transport vehicle for the children, a diesel Toyota
4x4 pickup, is all but dead after 6 years and over 350,000
miles of running through the bush. We desperately need reli-
able transportation. Like so many of us here in America these
days, when asked where the ends don't meet, the answer is,
we are beyond making them meet, we are just trying to hang
onto the pieces and take care of our kids until we can. We are
now facing the reality that we need several thousand dollars
just to keep the doors open and if we do not receive a financial
miracle in the next few weeks it could be the end of the project.
I have faith that God knows best.*

He asked for their financial support as well as their
prayers:

*Please help us pray for God's will to be made clear for the
future of the project and these children, for the unity and
strength of the staff, for the right partnerships and sponsors,
for funding, and for whatever comes next to be a testimony
of God's abundant love and grace toward all of us. Pray for
more volunteers in the United States to join the effort of
making this organization work. We need a few dedicated
believers with skills in multi-media, bookkeeping, education
and administration. Pray for the ones who have offered to
get involved. Pray for the grant writers and the donors. Pray
for me, a very unlikely candidate in very deep waters. Pray*

for my family, that the cycles that have been passed down for years will be broken and that every member will come to love the Lord and live in the victory He won when He died for us. I thank my God upon every remembrance of you.

This "unlikely candidate in very deep waters" would face difficult choices in the coming months. He had a grandson to raise. He had 350 children in Malawi and twenty project staff members to support and oversee. He had grave doubts about whether he could do both. He had just fired his longtime partner. He thought about Job. On the one hand, this was frightening, because he could face even greater challenges ahead. But on the other hand, it was reassuring: he didn't doubt for a minute that he would keep his faith in God.

Chapter 9

Breaking a Cycle

Driving along an empty country road in rural western North Carolina one winter evening, past fallow fields of tobacco and farmhouses with their kitchen lights revealing glimpses of family dinners, David Nixon opened up to me about how his time in Malawi had changed him and talked about the future of NOAH. I'd met him in Malawi in the fall of 2007, and since then, his life had taken many twists—twists of fate and twists of faith. He prayed he would go back to his project and perhaps live there full-time with Ethan, his now-six-year-old grandson. He burned to get back to Africa, but at the moment Africa was of less immediate importance than the boy in the back seat of his Cherokee who was humming a hymn about Jesus.

I took several trips during 2010 and 2011 to North Carolina, past the strip malls of Route 74, many of them with boarded-up stores and depressing empty parking lots, a visual drive-by of an economy that had fallen apart and spread ruin. Nixon and I had stayed in close touch since we met, but I needed to spend more time with him in North Carolina to fully understand his situation. I knew he was facing a critical moment in the future of the Malawi project, and he was agonizing over it. His e-mails were full of angst. Nixon had recently scaled back activities at NOAH. He still ran the feeding program for about 150 children and held some after-school classes, but he had suspended the full-time school operation and kept just a handful of staff. He had little choice: the economic crisis, starting in the summer of 2008, had taken a sizable toll on his fundraising. Churches gave less, and some once-reliable donors stopped giving altogether; one vital donor whom I would later meet had cut his substantial monthly gift in half. By 2008, Nixon had built up his project to a yearly budget of more than $150,000—well over $10,000 a month. Now, he was having trouble reaching $30,000 in a year.

A major reason for this was Ethan's presence in his life. The blond boy had become inquisitive, respectful, and playful (he loved to sing what Nixon called "Jesus songs" into his tape recorder and play them back to himself). He was not without his anxieties, and he threw tantrums from time to time, but by and large he had become a regular kid full of love for his grandfather and joy for his life. And that couldn't have made Nixon happier. He was raising Ethan in a stable home, and the boy seemed well adjusted. It was a blessing.

The big unanswered question—one that had been hanging over his head for more than a year now—was whether raising Ethan would mean giving up on Malawi. He still wanted to expand NOAH and return to his vision of a school that would provide an education and nourishing food for several hundred children.

Nixon was a storyteller, and I knew him well enough by this point that all I had to do was ask an open-ended question and let him talk. So as we started the drive to his home, I just asked how he was doing.

He reached back into his childhood to answer.

"God never planned for me to have the kind of childhood I had, but God is able to take that child who had that kind of life and turn it into something good. There's a way you can turn it around and help other children avoid that."

In just a few words, Nixon had explained what motivated him to go to Africa—and to rescue his grandson.

"So the way I grew up instilled a couple of things in me,"
he said. "The first thing was obviously a very, very tough will
to survive. The second thing was a great skepticism about
anybody and anything. It instilled in me a very intense ha-
tred for any kind of corrupt authority. It gave me a very keen
eye for what is good and true and right, and what is self-
serving. Now, it took me a long time to find the self-discipline
and resolve to live with all those things. The problem with a
very perceptive person is if you really live according to what
you believe, you have to turn that perception upon yourself.
You become your own worst critic. So for many years, that
was very difficult for me to reconcile. So I saw Christianity
the way I saw it originally, as a fourteen-year-old boy. It came
at an important time in my life and it had to be something
I could believe in. Really believe in it. Everything was riding
on it. It's my nature to scrutinize everything. If I decide to go
buy a laptop, I spend weeks researching laptops. So you can
only imagine then when I decide what religion am I going to
follow what I will do."

He laughed at himself. I joined in, and he laughed so
hard that tears sprang from his eyes. In his slightly self-
deprecating way, he had nailed himself, and both of us knew
it. But the point he made about what is self-serving stayed
with me. It made me think back to Ellen McCurley's comments about whether working in Africa was about saving
souls or saving your own soul. I couldn't help but think that
Nixon was trying to do both.

"The point in my life," he said finally, "is that God is
God, Satan is Satan, Jesus is real, and Jesus is the only way to
go. Now, trying to understand who is telling the truth about
Jesus is not so easy. I have read the Bible just for myself, for

months, studied it constantly. I learned a lot that I had never heard in church, never seen in church, the true nature of God, what it means to be a Christian, what it means to be a suffering servant, the true nature of congregational discipline, reading through the book of Proverbs, and understanding these are the ways a man should conduct himself. I am submitting to that, living in that moment."

We arrived at his new trailer about ten miles south of Monroe. His father had purchased it for him in the last year, and Nixon had bought seven acres around it, which included a section of woods. We went inside, and Nixon quickly prepared a meal for Ethan and himself; he said a prayer over the food, and the two of them ate. Within an hour, Ethan had washed his face, brushed his teeth, looked at a book in bed, listened to his grandfather talk about their plans for the following day as he was being tucked in, and then was sound asleep.

Nixon, too, felt exhausted. At the kitchen table, he rubbed his eyes and reflected on his new life with his grandson.

"In the beginning with Ethan, I never imagined it would lead to what it has," he said. "I had to seek the Lord for wisdom. It was another thing on my plate, but through God's perspective, it became clear that the number one ministry is my family. What good is it to help hundreds of children in Africa if my own flesh and blood is suffering? The Bible gives us clear guidance. In the book of Timothy, the qualification of being a leader in the body of the Lord is a man who is able to manage his own household well. You don't have an option to throw up your hands and say, 'My family is a mess, so let me go overseas where I can help.' The first priority is, have you done everything you absolutely can do for your own people first? Nothing is impossible. All things are possible. God tries to strengthen me.

When your priorities are out of whack, you no longer have God's blessing and purpose. If you get off on the wrong path, and things are not going well, you ask yourself, 'Is this a trial or am I running into obstacles because I'm not on the right path?' I am confident this is what God has planned for me."

But it wasn't so simple. When Nixon thought hard about it, he felt he had followed God's path, but that wasn't the end of the story. He admitted he faced lots of challenges in raising his grandson. In truth, nothing was easy in his life.

"The more I had transitioned into the full-time parent figure, not only does it become more difficult because of the day-to-day monotony, and it becomes more difficult to manage everything, but I've noticed this dynamic creeping in that was always there with my dad and still is," he said. "Everyone else who knows my dad thinks of him as a gentleman, very strong and outspoken to a degree, but never out of line. For those close to him, it's a completely different story. This is not unique to us. It's like people don't have this check that stops them from releasing their full anger, or a check that stops them from taking out their frustration on you.

"It's almost as if rather than loving people close to you, you hate them. They get the brunt of all of your stuff. I began to notice that coming into my relationship with Ethan. When I'm under the most incredible pressure, when I'm completely worn out, and because he's the one who is always there saying, 'Paw-Paw, I need clothes, I need food, I'm not happy, I don't like this. Tie my shoe, wipe my nose.' It's very easy to just go like, '*Kid!*' Since I never was around my children when they were small, I never experienced that. To feel that coming out of me was a real shock. It really disturbed me. I found myself thinking, *Why in God's name would I respond to Ethan in the same way that my father responded to me?* You have to understand there are things ingrained on you, imprinted on you as a small child, that you just don't decide that's not cool and it never happens again. That's a powerful thing that can manifest itself in a lot of powerful ways.

"Thank God I am not that type of person, or I don't want to be that type of person, and I recognize it when it starts to come out. But it still doesn't change the fact that it comes out almost automatically. The frustration. As I have wrestled with that and asked myself what goes into that, it's helped me to get an insight into my father that I never would have otherwise. Before I always looked at my dad and thought, *What's wrong with you? Why do you do that? Why do you blow up on people? Why are you so harsh sometimes? Why does it make me feel like you wish I would just go away? Why when I was a child whenever I was expecting any kind of relationship it was like 'Kid, get out of my face. Get out of my hair'?* I realize now that his behavior toward me was not an indicator of his genuine feelings for me; it was an indicator of how wounded he was. He went through some horrible things as a child. Really horrible, violent stuff. It's helped me to have more compassion and understanding.

"At the same time, having Ethan around is wearing off on my dad. If anything he's more and more tolerant and compassionate. The way he interacts with Ethan, I'm thinking, *God, I wish you had interacted with me that way.* But what also is happening is he's starting to get more and more comfortable, and he's relapsing more and more into his old self—his complaining and his outbursts. I'm really reluctant to confront him about it on the spot, with Ethan in the house because my dad is very unpredictable. I don't want to risk Ethan being exposed to that. It's a huge deal for me because I'm trying to overcome my childhood, I'm trying to break that cycle and have new patterns with Ethan, and to have him exposed to a completely different childhood." Nixon sighed. His face looked worn and haggard. It was time to go. I said good night and drove fifteen miles back to my hotel. On the way, I couldn't help but think about the choices Nixon faced with his grandson and with his Africa project, and his efforts to understand his past so that he could be something no one in his family had been: a loving father to a child. That exploration and that day-to-day reality took up so much of Nixon's energy and focus. He didn't say anything about what he would be doing with NOAH.

The next day, we met for lunch at a down-home restaurant in South Carolina, just over the North Carolina border, that served heaping plates of meat loaf and mashed potatoes and where the middle-aged waitresses called all men "hon." Nixon wanted me to meet a person who had been his largest benefactor for NOAH. His name was Perry Brown. He was worth millions from his years as a furniture wholesaler in Waxhaw, North Carolina, but Brown cultivated an aw-shucks style, especially with outsiders, that made him appear to be a humble country boy. He was anything but. Brown was a shrewd businessman and had founded his own Christian charity called Samaritans International, which was feeding children in Nicaragua, Haiti, Peru, Liberia, and, through NOAH, Malawi. Brown's charitable operation was centered in Nicaragua, where Samaritans International was feeding thirty thousand children a day. He was spending more than half his time there, and his heart was completely in the project.

But Brown and Nixon had a complicated relationship. For a while Brown was spending several thousand dollars a month contributing to NOAH's feeding program, and he had hired Nixon to do several large carpentry projects at his furniture business. But in 2009, Brown soured on Nixon and NOAH—Nixon thought it was because he didn't like the amount on an invoice for Nixon's carpentry work—and so Brown reduced his donation by half. Still, the two men saw each other fairly frequently, and Nixon often gave him reports on what was happening in Malawi.

Over lunch, I asked Brown what advice he had for Nixon in his Malawi operation. A sly smile spread over his face as he glanced from Nixon to me.

"That's the toughest question he's ever been faced with," Brown said, still smiling and seeming to enjoy the thought that Nixon was in a difficult spot. "The situation he is in, without the money to run this thing, I'd probably close it. He won't be able to have the teachers paid. He doesn't have the money to sustain the ministry. Other than that, I don't know. I have been praying that someone would take over the ministry or fully support the budget—and it's a pretty good budget, with the teachers, cooks. He's got a budget that is breaking his back. There's no way he could do it. I don't know where he is in it now. I just don't see how he's kept it as long as he has."

His smile still lingering, Brown returned to his mashed potatoes. Nixon showed no emotion. He seemed determined not to let Brown get to him. Brown was being honest, but he was clearly trying to get a rise out of Nixon.

"We closed the school temporarily at least," Nixon said.

"Did you?" Brown replied, not looking up.

"Yes, I told you I laid off a bunch of the teachers. I'm still doing a bunch of after-school programs in English and Bible studies, and that's after they go to the government school all day. The little ones still come for breakfast, and a lot of them come for lunch."

"How many teachers you have now?" Brown kept looking at his plate.

"Two," Nixon said. "They agreed to work as volunteers until we could pay them. They get health care, food, and a little bit of money, but not a teacher's salary. It's the only way we're surviving right now."

"He needs a miracle," Brown said, looking at me as if Nixon weren't there. "I hate to see those kids going hungry. You have to see it to believe it. He's been trying his best to come up with something for two years—and it just hasn't helped."

"This thing with Ethan has just handicapped me so bad," Nixon said. "It's eating up so much of my time and money. I used to be a single guy, keep my own schedule, live on a shoestring, and work day and night. It's completely changed now. You have to have money, you have to have health insurance, you have to pay lawyer's fees, day care—"

Brown cut him off. "I guess I would say he should find someone to turn the Malawi project over to."

"We've prayed for that," Nixon said. "I've told you, Perry, many times, I'd rather close the doors than give it to the wrong people."

"That's a tough one, though," Brown said, again addressing me, not Nixon. "He's trying to do the impossible. Of course, the impossible can be done." He laughed again. "It can be done. God can do anything. How many kids are we feeding there now?"

"One hundred fifty come without fail. We have three hundred sixty registered. At one time, we were feeding three thousand kids a day."

"Wow." Then Brown paid Nixon the only compliment I would hear from him: "You're tougher than I am."

Nixon laughed. "Oh, I don't know about that."

Brown picked up the check, and the two men parted. A few months later, Brown would cut funding down to a thousand dollars a month, and later he would cut it off entirely. He never gave Nixon a reason. I wasn't that surprised. Brown had his own agenda and his own long list of projects to fund. Clearly, something bothered him about Nixon. Maybe, with the dispute over the carpentry bills, Nixon had simply fallen out of favor with him, and Brown seemed like the type of person who wouldn't change his mind about someone after once sizing them up. I thought Nixon was probably better off without him as long as he could find new funding. That was a big *if*, of course. The children in Nixon's project would feel the impact of the departure of a major funder directly, in terms of meals and possibly schooling. It was a cautionary tale about the fickleness of giving and whether Americans could commit to a long-term project.

Nixon and I were now headed for another meeting that had the potential for tension: with his father, David Nixon Sr. I had wanted to meet the elder Nixon ever since his son told me the story about the slaughter of the bull. It wasn't that I expected to dislike him. But I looked forward to seeing how he would react to that story and whether he was capable, like his son was, of acknowledging past errors. I also wanted to hear what he thought of Nixon going to Malawi and now trying to balance raising Ethan and supporting his school in Africa. Did he admire his son, I wondered, for trying to break the family cycle?

The son had tried hard to repair his relationship with Senior over the past few years, and sometimes his efforts met with success. At times it was a joy, but often the elder Nixon would revert to his old ornery self. But early in 2010, during one of those difficult conversations, Nixon the son stopped his father in midsentence. Senior was complaining about members of the family and their issues, about how they weren't earning enough money, how they didn't take good enough care of themselves, how they didn't see him often.

"Dad, if you want to know why these things are happening, I can explain it if you'll listen to me," Nixon said.

Senior went quiet, and his son laid it all out for him, telling him that he, Senior, was as much to blame as anyone else for all the troubles.

"You married a young girl from Maryland and brought her to North Carolina, and then you went off on your truck," Nixon told his father that day. "Why should you be surprised that she didn't know how to keep house? Why should you be surprised that we don't behave as you wished?"

For three hours, the son talked and the father listened. The son felt he had made a breakthrough for just one reason: Senior didn't fight back. He didn't say anything. He just took it. And that made Nixon's visits to his father easier. They kept to a regular Sunday-morning breakfast at Senior's trailer. Senior would serve them a country breakfast of scrambled eggs and grits or pancakes. It was clear that Senior took great pleasure in these visits, and not just because he and his son had a better relationship; it was also because his great-grandson Ethan made him feel calmer and more relaxed. Ethan's enthusiasm and wonder were clearly a source of joy for Senior.

One Sunday, the then-five-year-old Ethan insisted that all three of them hold hands and pray together. Senior, who tended not to take part in the pre-meal prayer, was uncomfortable with the request, but he complied. A few weeks later, Ethan upped the ante. He said they all should hold hands and that it was Paw-Paw Nixon's—his name for Senior (he called Nixon just Paw-Paw)—turn to lead the prayer that day. Senior didn't hear the boy and asked him to repeat what he'd said. Ethan spoke up and Senior looked from his son to his great-grandson and said, "Well, I guess I can." He led them in prayer, and his son marveled at the moment.

But Nixon knew that maintaining the positive relationship with his father would be more difficult. "Some days I feel nothing but love and compassion and concern for him," he told me. "Other days, I go over there, and he's mad at the world, and when my father is mad, it's a whole different story. When he's in one of those moods, it draws up all those old feelings and reactions from my childhood. I start having a physical reaction—a headache, a knot in my stomach. I just get very quiet. After a while he picks up on the fact that I'm not talking, and he knows what I feel, so he starts backing off and changing his tune a little bit. I've started to see him as a human being, and while he would probably never admit it, he needs people the same as the rest of us do."

On the ride to his father's house, I wanted to know what Nixon was going to do if Brown stopped funding NOAH (which he would eventually do). One possibility was to bid for another USAID food-aid contract. But Nixon wasn't inclined to distribute so much food again, and, he said, Duncan Phiri and Zack Nkhata, who'd taken over after Jackson, did not want to renew the contract at the time.

"The resources to carry out that job—the logistics, the manpower—were enormous. It was a huge job for my staff. Most of the money was tied to the food. It did help us financially, but you also have to weigh how much time and effort it took out of us. We just weren't sure it was something we could sustain. It diverts your focus. If the focus is two to three hundred orphans, and if you are working night and day on food, protecting the inventory, it's taking time and energy away from what you want to do."

Nixon said he also had nagging feelings that the food aid did more harm than good. "There were people who lined up for food every day and they [became] dependent on the idea they are going to get food every day. They [came to feel] entitled to it. I don't like the idea of giving somebody food every day and becoming a source of food for them. They live in a place with a lot of water and a lot of land—very fertile land. Those resources could be used to teach them to grow their own food." I tended to agree with him. In fact, there were multiple problems in both emergency food aid and in distributing seeds to farmers. The former created a culture of dependency, while the latter was often done clumsily, destroyed the local market for seeds, and in the long run made it more difficult for farmers to purchase more seeds. Another unnecessary cost with U.S. food aid was a requirement that the food be purchased from American farmers, which added a huge bill for shipping the food to Africa.

Something else disturbed Nixon about the food distribution contract. The USAID contract required Nixon to disclose the budget and the number of children receiving food at every location. When Nixon went to Malawi to conduct interviews in the wake of the allegations against Jackson, he had stopped in at several of the feeding sites at the schools. He was initially pleased to hear that the sites were feeding many more children than the projections in the budget. Then he asked why.

"At the sites, they said they had a problem—they needed more food because they had twice as many children," Nixon told me. "I said, 'What are you doing about it?' They said they were giving every child half the meal. Then I asked, 'Why do you have twice as many children now?' And they told me that when families heard about the food distribution, they started sending all their children to the schools."

Drawing on his experiences at the NOAH school, Nixon understood immediately that this would create problems. "So then I started asking how many children per teacher there were when we signed up with them, and they said sixty to eighty children per teacher. So now they have twice the number of kids; do they have twice as many teachers? They said, 'No, sir, the government won't provide us with any more teachers.' So I had to ask again and put it in real terms. I asked if they now [had] a hundred and twenty children instead of sixty in a classroom, and they said, 'Yes, sir, that's what we are telling you.'"

Nixon shook his head as he drove. "So we have kids who were going to school for the right reasons before there was any food; they were getting a marginal education, at best. But because I brought this feeding program here and all these other children flocked to the school, they are not doing any education at all, really. What they described to me is really just crowd control. It became clear too that the government of Malawi was not going to provide more resources to meet the increase in the attendance, and teachers weren't going to turn any kids away. So I talked to the schools about it, and they agreed with me that the feeding program negatively affected kids' education. But then they said, 'They are getting more food and, better yet, they are starting to think about going to school. We want you to keep doing it.'"

For Nixon, this was all part of his learning experiences as an American trying to do good in Malawi. The learning was not limited to NOAH. He learned something about the unintended consequences of the food-distribution system he had used. It didn't sit well with him.

"Over the years of working in Malawi, I've come to some hard conclusions," he said as we approached his father's trailer, which was surrounded by bushes and sat on a hill overlooking barren fields. "One is there is really no good reason for those people to be as desperate as they are. When I go to these little farming villages, I say, 'Why aren't you growing food? Because the climate is right, the soil is right, you could be growing food right now.' Number one answer you get from people: 'It's not rainy season, we don't have water.' I've asked hydrologists about that and they say there is plenty of water in Malawi, that almost anywhere you drill you go down forty meters and you will hit some really good water. I know from my experience at NOAH that you can dig a ten- to twenty-meter well and get water. It may not be safe to drink, but you get water. I asked them why not hand dig wells for a family garden, but I can't get a straight answer.

"The other thing I hear from them: 'We don't have money for seed and fertilizer.' That's a different situation. They are largely dependent on the government for seed and fertilizer at a reasonable cost. But if people with horticultural experience go over there and teach them, they can learn to have sustainable farming. You can grow corn that will produce seed that you can use the next year. Other vegetables, same thing. There are ways to develop your own organic fertilizers."

I learned from talking to experts who worked in agricultural aid in Africa that Nixon was mostly right about the wells. The problem was that it cost money to dig wells, and most farmers or even communities didn't have the money for them. As for getting seed and fertilizer, it was more complicated than Nixon had let on. Researchers have been developing new hybrids of crops that, coupled with fertilizers, can produce great yields. But again, that costs money. Still, Nixon was learning more and more from his experiences in the field and from listening to Africans and not stubbornly clinging to preconceived notions he'd taken with him on his first flight to Africa. He had no ulterior motives. He just thought that any development project should produce intended results, and if it didn't, it shouldn't continue. His answers wouldn't help the project—at any rate, they hadn't yet. As he described himself, he was a problem solver, and this was a problem that could be solved. At least that's what he thought. And what was the answer to Africa's widespread poverty? He was leading up to just that in the car.

"I've come to a point where I've started to realize that even more than I did in the beginning, education is really the key to everything," he said. "Worldwide seed and fertilizer programs are not the answer. Monsanto is not going to feed the world. They are not going to get any bigger than they are, not going to get any richer, and they are still not feeding the world. They are feeding off gigantic farmers, but they are not feeding the local farmer. So those who really need food are not benefiting. The answer to rural people in developing countries is sustainable small-scale farming. That, plus much better education for all the children."

He had a great point about education and small-scale farming. Small-scale farmers were the way ahead. It reminded me of the old Lao Tzu poem that says in part:

> *Go to the people*
> *Live with them*
> *Learn from them*
> *Love them*
> *Start with what they know*
> *Build with what they have.*

In other words, start with the existing system of farmers, add technical expertise, and those farmers should reap the benefits. Africa was full of children with poor education and farmers with poor crops. Governments in Africa needed to invest in both, and faith-based U.S. groups could assist them, especially if they stayed away from spending exorbitant amounts of money on orphanages, which did nothing to solve the deficit of proper education.

We got out of Nixon's car and headed for his father's trailer. Senior had come to his front stoop to greet us. He wore a baseball cap, slacks, and a long-sleeved shirt buttoned at the wrists. He was taller than his son, and when he shook my hand, his hand nearly swallowed mine. He was over six feet tall, well into his eighties, and starting to be slowed by age and disease. His eyes were misty, and he wore hearing aids. He had prostate cancer, high blood pressure, and low-grade diabetes, and he had suffered a stroke a few years before.

I didn't know if my visit with Senior would be that memorable. Nixon had told me that his father's mind jumped from one subject to another and that he tended to steer all conversation toward a handful of topics. One was the economy and the high cost of a gallon of gas; it wasn't a surprise that a former long-distance truck driver still had his mind on the gas pump. Another topic was taxes; he railed against them as easily as he drew breath. Nixon warned me that his father had a racist streak in him; when he started on that topic, the son would always excuse himself and leave. "Anytime he goes down the path, I start boiling inside. I have to go," Nixon said. But Senior had a soft spot for his son and great-grandson, Nixon said. He loved Ethan, probably more than he cared to admit.

Senior invited us inside. I sat on a couch close to him. He slowly lowered himself into a recliner, which had an unobstructed view of a huge TV across the living room. I introduced myself, but he cut me off. "You have to speak up," he said. And I nearly shouted to him, "What do you think about your son in Africa?"

"He's helping people," Senior said. "I know those children need an education, a place to stay; their parents can't do it because they can't afford to do it. It's a poor nation. What I can't understand is why there are so many children. I know David and Perry Brown—he's involved too—have been in it, and it's all good to go around and get donations from people here. But most of the people over here can't donate because they got to make their own living. That's got to do with the tax people. A lot of people can't afford to pay their own taxes, but they raise the taxes up."

I tried to steer the conversation to his son and said that it seemed like he hadn't had much of a relationship with him until recently.

"They didn't see the hardship we had to have when we grew up," he said with a note of defensiveness. "I had nothing. Nobody could help me. I had to do it myself. When I was traveling, sometimes I'd get home six times a year. Once you are gone, it's hard to pick up on things. I knew what was right, what was wrong, but it was a little too late to impress on them, too late to teach them when they get older. But David, he's taking care of his grandson now, he's teaching him now the best way."

I couldn't help myself. I asked him about the Jersey bull that he'd shot in front of his son.

"The bull?" he said, looking puzzled. "Bull?"

His son, sitting across the room, briefly explained.

"Oh," he said. "Well, it was just a calf. I don't remember it."

I let it go. I had already ventured into an uncomfortable area for Senior, and if it did indeed stir a memory, he didn't say so.

So we started talking about Nixon's decision to raise Ethan. "It's good what he did, but he's taking on a lot of responsibility," Senior said. "He shouldn't have to do it, but it's something that has to be done. David comes over for breakfast with Ethan. I don't mind at all. David's teaching him right and wrong."

I had one other question for him. I couldn't tell how he really felt about his son and great-grandson. Senior didn't seem one to delve into his feelings except on things that he didn't like. In fact, he really only liked to talk about things that he disagreed with. So I asked him what his favorite time of the week was.

He sat there thinking. His eyes focused on the mid-distance; they seemed to be a little watery. I started to ask the question again, but he waved me off. He had heard me the first time.

"I guess it's having Ethan over here, eating breakfast, playing with his toys," Senior said, and his eyes were misty. "It's every Sunday morning. That's really the only company I have. I lost my hearing. I'm brain dead when I can't hear. I don't like to be around people where I don't know what they are saying. Rather not be there."

Nixon stood to leave. I thanked Senior for seeing me. When Nixon and I drove off, I mentioned that what Senior said about Ethan was nice.

"Yes, it was," Nixon said. "I hadn't heard that before."

The next day, we drove out to see someone who would help me put Nixon's decision in perspective—his mother. We decided to meet her halfway between her house and

Nixon's, in a tiny town called Waxhaw, which, in addition to being home to Perry Brown's wholesale furniture business, was a tourist town, even if it was quite remote.

We met Elizabeth Bridges on Waxhaw's main street. Railroad tracks split the town in two, with antique stores, a couple of coffee shops, and other storefronts on either side of the tracks. We picked a coffee shop and sat down. Bridges was seventy-one, but she looked much younger. She immediately started telling the story of her son coming into one of her classes to talk about NOAH.

"The students were just stunned—especially about the material around the funeral of Sautso," she said. "It made them stop and think how good they have it."

"I just showed that video to a group of potential volunteers a few weeks ago, and I lost it again," Nixon said. "It tapped into something very deep in myself. I have to get over it. I have to find a way to get past it."

"Well, you know, David, what comes to mind is the helplessness, because you were helpless," Bridges told her son. "You did everything you could do and it wasn't enough. That's the way it was with their lives. In that dysfunctional family in Africa, you can do everything you can do and it's not enough. You can't fix it."

"It makes you feel tired," Nixon said. "It makes you wonder why you should do it at all if it's going to end up like that. You can logically acknowledge that's not the reality; there are a lot of children who have been helped there. But still there is something deep that happened there. Sometimes your logical process is not enough to overcome it."

Bridges said she had had a somewhat similar experience when she worked with young women at a halfway house. "One girl is upset with me because we are not doing the amount of services that we used to do," she said. "It relates back to how David might feel when it comes to Sautso. Okay, so he has fed a lot of children in Africa; he's seen to it there is water not just for them but for children in nearby villages, so he has made a lot of difference. So if there is one person you can't save, you take that very hard. If you can't save Sautso, it is very disheartening."

Nixon was visibly shaken. "If you're right there when it's happening, when he's dying, and you know all the best people in the country, and still the child dies right under your nose, it really takes the wind out of you," he said. "And then your longest-running, seemingly most faithful staff member is found to be corrupt and doing things you never dreamed of. It's just a horrible one-two punch. You can tell yourself consciously, 'Good people there, a good cause, and I'm still needed and still effective,' but you are only human. If you are deeply wounded, you are deeply wounded."

"When I'm wounded like that, it taps into the old wounds," his mother said. "It's probably true with you too."

Nixon nodded. "I kind of look at it like this: There's a purpose for suffering in our lives. The Lord allows these things to happen for a purpose. My reasoning is God has used these series of events to draw up these old issues from my past so they can be dealt with, so I can overcome them. They are extremely difficult to face. Yesterday, I was becoming almost disoriented. I am bringing all these things to a head. In some respects, I have been paralyzed. I've had Sautso, Africa, Jackson, my own son, my grandson. My goodness. Truth is, God's grace is sufficient. All of it has to be brought up so I could overcome it. Otherwise it is going to continue to overcome me the rest of my life. I have to overcome it. You certainly agree, most people cover up old wounds and they don't go away. They have to be dealt with."

His mother was nodding. "If you don't deal with those things, they will jump up and bite you at the most inopportune time," she said.

They laughed. Bridges started talking about her son's decision to raise Ethan.

"It's positive, but it's also heartbreaking. I see the same thing happening with David's son as I saw happening with David," Bridges said. "David's son steps up to the plate, gets things straightened out, then goes back down again. The children are suffering for it. I believe David is breaking a cycle in a family where fathers have abandoned their children. My father abandoned my family. My children never really had a father. Even when David [Senior] lived with the family, he was never there. If he wasn't off trucking, he was off drinking and gambling. He was never there. I told David that what he did with Ethan, he was breaking a cycle. I see him setting aside everything that is dear to him—Africa first and foremost and the dedication he has been able to have with Africa, had to set it aside to a great degree. He hasn't been able to do anything like he used to do before he had Ethan. I see him giving up something he loves for something he loves more. For something he believes in. And doing it for a little boy who, if David doesn't do it, there isn't anybody who is going to do it. If David doesn't keep him, you might as well throw him in the middle of a highway, because he wouldn't stand a chance. Because he is doing what he is doing with Ethan, Ethan is getting what nobody in this family has ever gotten. That is somebody who is willing to give up their life to see to it that the child has a life."

That did it. The two of them were in tears. Bridges had told her son that letting go of a project that he had embraced with more energy and passion than anything before in his life was the right thing to do. As hard as it might have been for Nixon to believe over the past two years, his mother was telling him that he had sacrificed himself and his Africa project for the good of one child. And after losing a child in Africa, if he could save a child here, it was the right thing to do. Nixon looked at his mother. "If there is anybody I've got to thank, it's you," he said.

As he tended to do when overcome with emotion, Nixon wanted to shift the focus from himself and talk about his faith. "You know, one of the biggest perils of ministry is doing it for someone else. You have to be doing it for the Lord. He has to be it. It can't ever be to please your mother, your father, your pastor, anybody. You can't allow what other people think of you to affect your life. The Holy Spirit wants to be the controller of your life. He wants to be the director. If you are devastated by someone like Jackson, or Sautso, you have to deal with those feelings, but ultimately that can't direct what you do the next day. You have to be directed by what the Holy Spirit tells us to do. A lot of people who go to Africa, a lot of them are Christians and they want to be in ministry. Well, you have to have some character to be in ministry. Because if you don't, you are going to go down. If you are not doing it for the right motives and the Lord hasn't built some character in you, you are going to get discouraged at the first thing, or you are going to give up when things don't go well. I think that's what the Bible means when it says lay hands suddenly on no man [1 Timothy 5:22]. Let people be grounded in the word of God, let people be deep in their relationship with the Lord before they go to Africa to make a difference."

"People are very sincere when they start, but they often don't follow through," his mother told him. "All through the Scripture it says count the costs before you start to build the building."

Nixon laughed. "Well, who goes out to build a tower and doesn't count the costs and then in the end the tower is unfinished? Me!"

They laughed some more. "You have to trust God for the results," Nixon said.

We walked out into Waxhaw and its slow-paced ways. Mother and son hugged, and after lingering together for a few moments, they drove off in separate directions. In Nixon's Cherokee, I asked him what was next. I said that it seemed to me that everyone in his life was either directly or subtly saying that he should let the Malawi project go. Would he?

He was silent for several moments. "Sorry," he said, finally. "It's just a lot to think about. But I think leaving Malawi is not an option. It goes to the very core of who I am, why I do the things I do, my whole worldview."

It was obviously a critical decision. If Nixon left, he would be like many Americans who started these projects, helped people, raised their expectations, and then dashed them. Countries like Malawi are full of people who had relationships with Americans who helped them for a while and then let them down. Americans could say that things happened, that life changed. It was true, of course, that Ethan needed his grandfather. But from the African perspective, when an American walked away, it meant a relationship severed, a perceived compact broken, not to mention the loss of material support that the Africans had come to depend on. So there is justifiable wariness on the side of many Africans because of these experiences. They were right to question whether Nixon would really live up to his word and stay for the long haul.

Nixon said that for years he had listened to people tell him that working in Malawi was a noble thing to do but that he didn't really have to make it his goal in life.

"There is wisdom in many counselors," he said, "but ultimately the final word has to come from God. I really do not believe God has done everything he has done in Malawi, and in my life, for me to close the book on that and walk away. I believe that is what I'm being tempted to do. That's not just based on my perception of the situation. That is based on the reality that I still see God intervening in Malawi on a regular basis. Every time I say to the Lord, 'Do you want me to wrap this up, and focus on Ethan, and focus on my business, focus on becoming a reasonably respected individual, rather than this poor missionary who is stressed so bad he can't think straight?' the answer I get is 'I'm not done yet. Wait on me. Be still and know that I am the Lord.'"

So he would be still.

As hard as that would be, he would do it. Nixon said that was the biggest lesson for him. He could make plans, he could raise funds, he could raise a six-year-old boy in a rural North Carolina town all the while wondering why he wasn't helping 350 boys and girls get meals and a proper education every day in a Malawian village. Or he could accept that God had a plan for him. He believed there had to be a balance, but part of that balance for him was believing that ultimately God would show him the proper path.

The path, he fervently believed at that moment, would lead him back to Malawi.

"The story is not over," he said, laughing, his voice rising. He looked over at me, grinning as he drove on the empty road. "I can guarantee you that. It's not over."

Acknowledgments

I have many people to thank. First, there are those who gave so much time to me in telling their stories. David Nixon tops my list. He showed extraordinary patience in putting up with thousands of questions and all of my visits to see him in Malawi and North Carolina. Ellen McCurley, who founded the Pendulum Project that supports community groups in Malawi, has been a wise guide and friend. Kerry Olson, the founder of the Firelight Foundation, spent many hours with me talking about the benefits of community-based aid. Several others allowed me to spend days, and sometimes weeks, with them in the field, including Jacques Jackson in Malawi; Nasir al-Amin in Addis Ababa, Ethiopia; Steve and Dianne Warn in Kisumu, Kenya; Dave and Melissa Osborn in Nairobi, Kenya, and in their home in Oklahoma City; Dan and Patty Schmelzer in Kisumu, Kenya; Vickie Winkler in Nairobi, Kenya; and Annie Duguid in Kampala, Uganda.

I could not have written this book without the financial support of the Kaiser Family Foundation as a media fellow during 2007 to 2008 and the continuous encouragement from the foundation's inestimable Penny Duckham. Journalists and writers around the world are indebted to Penny. I'd also like to thank several people at the *Boston Globe* for their support of my coverage of AIDS and global health generally, including editor Marty Baron, who made the courageous decision to devote scarce resources to the coverage of global health over several years during my postings in Washington and South Africa; foreign editor Jim Smith, for his wisdom and grace; other editors on the *Globe's* Foreign Desk who offered consistent encouragement, including David Beard, Richard Chacon, Ken Kaplan, and Roy Greene; and longtime colleague Sally Jacobs, who helped me find new avenues in my reporting and writing.

Many U.S. government experts on AIDS and orphans were generous with their time and expertise, including ambassadors Randall Tobias, Dr. Mark Dybul, and Jimmy Kolker; Beverly Nyberg; Caroline Ryan; Michelle Maloney-Kitts; Thomas Kenyon; Warren "Buck" Buckingham; Gray Handley; Kevin De Cock; Tom Walsh; Jennifer Peterson; Kristin Pugh; Elissa Pruett; Nicole Schiegg; and Amy Black.

My agent, Sam Stoloff, vice president and senior agent at Frances Goldin Literary Agency in New York City, not only found a wonderful home for this book at Beacon Press but also helped me shape the structure of the narrative. Sam was my teacher.

My two editors—Amy Caldwell, executive editor at Beacon, and her assistant, Will Myers—set me straight too many times to mention. They were thoughtful, challenging, creative, and kind. This book has much of them in it. Copy editor Tracy Roe's careful editing was first rate.

On the road, I traveled with photographer Dominic Chavez to collect many of these stories. He and his wife, artist Silvia Lopez Chavez, helped make this idea of a book come true. Dominic and I shared Tuskers, St. Georges, Guinnesses, and even Kuche Kuches after long days of reporting, and over all of them he shared his clear-eyed insights into many of the characters in this book.

Finally, I'd like to thank my wonderful wife, Laura Hambleton, a writer, editor, and filmmaker, for her encouragement, patience, and humor; and I'd like to thank our three children, Paige, Gavin, and Wyatt. I always hurried back to them after spending time with orphans in Africa.

A Note on Sources

For this book, I interviewed more than two hundred people who were connected in some way with efforts to help children in Africa. For the reporting, I traveled to South Africa, Malawi, Kenya, Uganda, Ethiopia, and Rwanda, as well as to several states in the United States, including North Carolina, California, and Oklahoma. For all scenes in which I use quotations, I was either physically present or, if the scene occurred prior to the start of my reporting, relied on at least two people who were present. In a few cases, mostly from David Nixon's early years, I relied on Nixon and his family members.

For those readers who want suggestions on ways to help children in Africa, there are many groups doing great work. I will bring up just three that I observed firsthand.

First, there is David Nixon's NOAH. By now, readers can judge for themselves whether the project is something they would support. The best way to reach Nixon is by e-mail (director@thenoahproject.org) or regular mail (2914 Ruben Road, Monroe, North Carolina 28112).

The second is Ellen McCurley's Pendulum Project, which is also working in Malawi. The project funds small community-based projects that support families. For more information, send an e-mail to ellenmcc@comcast.net or

look at the website of the project's U.S. fiscal agent, the Face
to Face Aids Project, www.facetofaceaids.org.

And the third is the Firelight Foundation, a public charity that provides small grants to grassroots organizations in
Africa that are addressing the needs of children and families
made vulnerable by poverty and HIV and AIDS. For more
information, see www.firelightfoundation.org.